I

S U R

R E N

D E R

To order additional copies of *I Surrender,* by DuWayne Carlson,
call 1-800-765-6955.

Visit us at **www.reviewandherald.com** for information
on other Review and Herald® products.

I SURRENDER

DU WAYNE A. CARLSON

ᴙR

REVIEW AND HERALD® PUBLISHING ASSOCIATION
Since 1861 | www.reviewandherald.com

Review and Herald® titles may be purchased in bulk for educational, business, fund-raising, or sales promotional use. For information, e-mail SpecialMarkets@reviewandherald.com.

The Review and Herald® Publishing Association publishes biblically based materials for spiritual, physical, and mental growth and Christian discipleship.

The author assumes full responsibility for the accuracy of all facts and quotations as cited in this book.

Unless otherwise noted, all Scripture references are from the *Holy Bible, New International Version*. Copyright © 1973, 1978, 1984, 2011 by Biblica, Inc. Used by permission. All rights reserved worldwide.

Texts credited to Clear Word are from *The Clear Word,* copyright © 1994, 2000, 2003, 2004, 2006 by Review and Herald Publishing Association. All rights reserved.
Texts credited to Message are from *The Message.* Copyright © 1993, 1994, 1995, 1996, 2000, 2001, 2002. Used by permission of NavPress Publishing Group.
Texts credited to NKJV are from the New King James Version. Copyright © 1979, 1980, 1982 by Thomas Nelson, Inc. Used by permission. All rights reserved.
Bible texts credited to RSV are from the Revised Standard Version of the Bible, copyright © 1946, 1952, 1971, by the Division of Christian Education of the National Council of the Churches of Christ in the U.S.A. Used by permission.
Bible texts credited to TNIV are from the *Holy Bible, Today's New International Version.* Copyright 2001, 2005 by International Bible Society. Used by permission of International Bible Society. All rights reserved worldwide.

Statements in this volumn attributed to other speakers/writers are included for the value of the individual statements only. No endorsement of those speakers'/writers' other works or statements intended or implied.

This book was
Edited by Raymond H. Woolsey
Copyedited by Delma Miller
Cover designed by Daniel Anez / Review and Herald® Design Center
Cover photo © Thinkstock.com
Typeset: 11/13 Minion Pro

PRINTED IN U.S.A.

18 17 16 15 14   5 4 3 2 1

Library of Congress Control Number: 2013954537

ISBN 978-0-8280-2732-8

ACKNOWLEDGMENTS

The Holy Spirit has influenced my mind through the works of many different people, including the following. Allister Becht, in a Moody Bible Radio broadcast that dealt with God giving the children of Israel the Ten Commandments after they left Egypt, started my thinking on this subject. Sermons by David Smith and Ron Carlson, as well as books by Max Lucado, Ellen White, and, most important, the Bible, have influenced my thoughts along the way.

I thank the editor of my first manuscript (which actually has little resemblance to the current), Marcia Claesson.

I thank my friend Chris Blake for reading my initial manuscript and then sitting down over breakfast and giving me a one-hour College Writing 101 synopsis.

Herbert Douglass, a friend from many years ago, has been a great help in reading the present manuscript and giving experienced advice. Invaluable!

Ann Halim has poured countless hours into putting my gibberish into readable language. I know editing this was a nightmare. Thank you so much, Ann!

I thank my children, who have consented to having stories about them included here, as well as tolerating Dad's "one-string violin" of learning to depend on God.

Karen—my wife, cheerleader, reality checker, friend, editor, and blessing from the Lord—thanks!

I thank God for guiding my thoughts and then prompting me to write them down in this book. More than anything, I thank Him for allowing me to have this understanding, as it has greatly affected my relationship with Him. It has given me hope when I have felt that my sins and continued failures have been too great to be forgiven. I humbly present this manuscript as His.

CONTENTS

This world appears to be spiraling out of control. Terrorism and intimidation through the threat of nuclear weapons, economic failure of corporations and governments, hunger and famine, increasingly frequent freakish disasters, weird changes in the climate, HIV and swine flu epidemics along with possible other pandemics, business and government fraud, escalating crime, and environmental devastation. Are we drawing to the close of our earth's history?

While we don't know if this is the time and hour, we would like to have some assurance that things are going to be OK, now and in the future. We don't want to be worried about the perilous times of the last days. What should we be doing? Storing up food, building secluded shelters in the mountains, or something else?

We crave relief when facing tragedy and uncertainty. Some choose chemical substances to numb the pain and worry. Some hold on to relationships and family to get them through. Others worry incessantly about safety—their own and that of their loved ones. A few have a belief system that anchors them.

God told us through Paul, "Do not be anxious about anything" (Phil. 4:6). Anything? Yes, *anything*. Do not be anxious about terrorists obtaining nuclear weapons. Do not be anxious about employment, finances, or even what to eat in this economy turned sour. Do not be anxious about your family's safety or even your own. Do not be anxious about *anything!* A tall order perhaps, but exactly what God wants from us.

As we pore through Scripture, we see individuals who completely and fully depended on God—heroes of faith such as Joseph, Daniel, and above all, Jesus. In stark contrast we read the heart-wrenching stories of Cain, King Saul, and Balaam—those who failed miserably because they refused to trust God with all their heart. Our hope is rekindled as we study Abraham, David, Paul, and Peter, and watch them move from autonomy to a posture of dependence as they observe God's leading in their experience. Dependence on God is at the heart of what He wants from each of us.

CHAPTER 1

HOW CAN DEPENDENCE BE A GOOD THING?

INDEPENDENCE, THE HUMAN CONDITION

Mine was the dubious task of finding a new home, and the clock was ticking. Karen, my wife, was not very happy about this move. Not only would she be leaving her hometown, but we were moving away from the new house we had planned, built, and just recently moved into. It was the place we had dreamed of staying at until our kids were grown. Now circumstances had changed, and the orthopedic practice I joined was not working out the way I had envisioned. Decisions had been made that were compromising patient care, and I could not, in good conscience, stay. A move to Phoenix was the best of all the available job options, and so here I was, looking for a place to live. Our budget was tight because we had not yet sold our recently built home.

Wearily I scrutinized property after property with the realtor. Each one was either too expensive or too shabby. I knew Karen wouldn't be excited about a dilapidated house in a run-down area, yet our budget kept reminding me that the nicer homes were out of our reach.

After the realtor left, I was driving around a lovely neighborhood, up one street and down another, looking for sale signs. *Lord, I need help! You know where there is a house we can afford and one that Karen will find acceptable. Please help me find the right spot.*

Just then I turned down a cul-de-sac and noticed a woman and her daughter walking out of a house and getting into their car. I quickly stopped and inquired whether they knew of any houses in the area that might be going up for sale soon.

A quizzical look came across the daughter's face as she glanced toward her mother. It turned out the two of them were moving the daughter's belongings out of the house to a new place in preparation for her upcoming marriage. Since she was the youngest of the family, her mom and dad were going to move to a smaller house. Their home was going to be on the market in a week or two, and yes, they were interested in selling it. I eagerly waited as Karen and the children surveyed the home, then quietly rejoiced when Karen approved. God blessed, and the asking price qualified us for a loan until our other home sold.

I had cried out to God and depended on His ability to work out the situation, and He had come through yet again. That was in 1996. Since then He has blessed innumerous times.

God is always with us. He doesn't respond only when we are in deep weeds and need help—He craves our constant dependence. Sometimes we don't really want to make that much commitment. We want to be independent. We want help only when we can't handle it on our own.

Recently I offered to pray with a patient before surgery. As an orthopedic trauma surgeon, I often care for people who are in frightening situations with unplanned injuries. Each patient's life is altered significantly in the short term, and often the residual effects in the long term. Before surgery, I usually approach patients with, "I am not sure where you are with this, and it is OK if you do not want to participate, but I would be willing to have prayer with you if you would like."

This particular patient was about 27 years of age, and when I offered to pray with him, he stated, "I don't have a problem with you praying, but I really don't need it." In other words, *I can handle this one on my own. Yeah, God is up there and I don't have a problem with you praying if you need it, but I am just fine on my own.*

Human beings have long held independent living as a highly sought-after value. The thought of dependence is downright repulsive to many. The pioneering spirit that sent caravans west, roughing it on the frontier, relying on willpower and stamina, remains memorialized, especially in the minds of the young and adventurous.

Beginning in infancy and extending to the grave, we are steeped in self-sufficiency. After birth, we mark the milestones—sitting up, walking unassisted, going to the bathroom alone, and dressing without help. Ever try feeding or dressing an independent 2-year-old? "I do it myself!"—even when the task is greater than the child's abilities. We are infected with the spirit of independence from a very young age.

Toddlerhood is about learning, experiencing, and accomplishing tasks independently. Throughout the school-age years, those independent skills are further developed until adolescence begins emerging. Then, not only are skills done independently, but the parent's ethics and thought processes are challenged and one's own philosophy, worldview, and goals are solidified independently.

With the adult years comes the pursuit of financial independence. The more financially successful one becomes, the more independent he or she is considered in the fiscal arena—an enviable position to most. Some who are exceptionally financially independent attempt to pass on to their children through early scholastic training, the ability—and responsibility—for early success and the child's own financial independence.

Even old age is fraught with issues of autonomy. The elderly strive to hold on to their independence. Driving, going to the store, living in their own home rather than a nursing home, and many other independent activities are treasured.

This developmental moving and staying independent from other people is necessary to an extent, but it remains imperative that we be dependent on God.

DEPENDENCE IS COUNTERCULTURAL

Any journey toward dependence is very countercultural, as independence is generally valued. "Dependence" is not a pleasing or comfortable word. It applies to people not capable of fending for themselves or not able to function without the help of someone more knowledgeable or capable. Dependence is scorned, and people work to avoid being associated with this form of need.

"Dependence describes those that do not have it together, and I don't want to be like that."

"If I am depending on someone else, I am not in control. If I am not in control, things just won't get done or won't get done the right way, my way."

"I would be relying on someone else, and their plans may get in the way of my plans, dreams, and goals."

Tim Stafford writes, "We cannot easily accept absolute, eternal dependence. It is the ultimate insult to our pride" ("Knowing the Face of God," by Tim Stafford, in *NIV Men's Devotional Bible*, p. 115. Copyright 1986 by Tim Stafford, Zondervan Publishing House. Used by permission).

Presently, almost everything is oriented toward "being my own person," doing it the way I want, pleasing myself on my schedule. Someone looking for dependence on God may feel out of touch and be pressured into the mold of personal goals, personal plans, and personal priorities. Financial goals, educational goals, status goals—these are set so we can feel good about our accomplishments and our growing independence. Even within the church, goals are set for this and that—sometimes even the number of souls to be won. Where does dependence on God come in?

DEPENDENCE, THE HEAVENLY EXAMPLE

Let us contrast our independent bent with the Example we were given of dependence. If there was ever an individual who was qualified for an independent life, it was Jesus. He knew the goals for His stay on earth. He had all power available at His fingertips, but He chose a different path, to show how we can overcome the devil through dependence on God. He showed us that through true dependence, the battle with the devil can be won, even under what seems to be overwhelming odds.

"By myself I can do nothing; I judge only as I hear, and my judgment is just, for I seek not to please myself but him who sent me" (John 5:30).

"For I have come down from heaven not to do my will but to do the will of him who sent me" (John 6:38).

"My teaching is not my own. It comes from the one who sent me" (John 7:16).

"The words I say to you I do not speak on my own authority. Rather, it is the Father, living in me, who is doing his work" (John 14:10).

"If you keep my commands, you will remain in my love, just as I have kept my Father's commands and remain in his love" (John 15:10).

Though He was qualified to live a life of autonomy, these texts make it clear that independence was not Jesus' goal. Rather, dependence was the central theme of His life because He knew He could—and would—be a conqueror through it. These texts state that everything He said and did was directed from the Father. He had total confidence that His Father would not allow anything to happen that was not for the best good of His mission on earth. The devil could try anything he wanted, but he was not allowed to interrupt the plan and mission for Jesus' life. With this confidence, Jesus was at complete peace in all circumstances, even in the face of apparent danger—He knew the Father's watch care was over Him.

Think of the time the storm came up on the Sea of Galilee, and the disciples feared for their lives.

"Absorbed in their efforts to save themselves, they had forgotten that Jesus was on board. . . . In their helplessness and despair they cried, 'Master, Master!' . . . When Jesus was awakened to meet the storm, He was in perfect peace. There was no trace of fear in word or look, for no fear was in His heart. But He rested not in the possession of almighty power. It was not as the 'Master of earth and sea and sky' that He reposed in quiet. That power He had laid down, and He says, 'I can of Mine own self do nothing' (John 5:30). He trusted in the Father's might. It was in faith—faith in God's love and care—that Jesus rested, and the power of that word which stilled the storm was the power of God.

"As Jesus rested by faith in the Father's care, so we are to rest in the care of our Savior. If the disciples had trusted in Him, they would have been kept in peace. Their fear in the time of danger revealed their unbelief. In their efforts to save themselves, they forgot Jesus; and it was only when, in despair of self-dependence, they turned to Him that He could give them help" (*The Desire of Ages*, pp. 334-336).

The best example of Jesus' dependence is shown in how He traversed from Gethsemane to Calvary. Complete dependence on the Father was the only way Jesus was able to negotiate this struggle while maintaining not only a tolerance for His persecutors but a true and genuine love. "When they hurled their insults at him, he did not retaliate; when he suffered, he made no threats. Instead, he entrusted himself to him who judges justly" (1 Peter 2:23).

Jesus knew that everything happening to Him had a reason—to show either earthlings or the inhabitants of the remainder of the universe the true character of God versus that of Satan. Though He could not see it immediately, everything that happened that day was either to win or retain souls for the kingdom. Because He knew "all things worked together for good," He could endure the pain, suffering, and, worst of all, the separation from His Father. He was sustained by His unlimited trust and dependence on God.

The devil knew that dependence was at the center of Christ's success. The three temptations he threw at Jesus in the wilderness tried to attack that dependence and get Christ to step away from it.

If You are the Son of God, tell these stones to become bread.

If You are the Son of God, throw Yourself down.

All of this I will give You *if* You bow down and worship me.

These temptations, these disguised accusations, were intended to entice Jesus into doubt and ultimately into independence from His single-minded goal of doing only what He saw the Father doing. In effect, the devil was declaring: 1. Do it Yourself; You have the power. Besides, God is not providing for You. 2. God will provide. Just jump off and force His hand a little. Don't listen for instructions; break out and show me You are His Son. 3. Avoid the pain that's coming; dependence is going to be painful. You will be deserted by all, including Your Father. Do it the easy way and reach Your goal without His guidance. I will give it to You; just worship me.

The devil presents these same three temptations in varying forms to us. He still tempts us with "go ahead and do it yourself. You don't need any help with this. Besides, God will get in the way of doing it your way."

There are insidious ways that the devil tries to get us to "go ahead and do it yourself." It might take the form of borrowing money to make a large purchase such as a new car, television, home, boat. "We are putting the lender in the place of God. Who needs God to provide for us when someone will lend to us?" ("Master Your Money," by Ron Blue, in *NIV Men's Devotional Bible*, p. 771. Copyright 1986 by Ron Blue, Thomas Nelson Publishers).

Even for those who are more "spiritual," there are temptations: "Step out in faith. If you don't step out of your usual modus operandi, God will never be able to act in your favor." Yes, stepping out in faith is important if you are sure that it is by the prompting of the Holy Spirit.

However, often someone tries to be the Holy Spirit for another. Have you ever heard, "You need to step out in faith for the Lord to bless"? Usually it is in connection with a church-related project for which the finances are not available to begin the process. Someone who wants this project off the ground encourages others to "proceed in faith." If we push forward under the presumptuous temptation of "proceeding with faith" when we were not providentially asked to do so, we may experience disastrous effects. Instead, we need to truly depend on Him, not what we would like to push His hand to do through us.

The third temptation is just to go the easy way. This is particularly effective for those bombarded with trials, or perhaps those who are just basically lazy spiritually.

I have been running with my son Brad for several years, helping him train for cross-country racing, other road races, and most recently for endurance events. Early on, I mainly trained for exercise, as well as to help Brad in his pursuits. Often when I run, the thought of being exhausted at the end of the run slows me down or may even prompt me to choose a shorter mileage. When I have already run four or more miles of one hill after another, the sight of one more incline makes me almost want to quit; the effort is just too much, even though I may be only mildly winded and nowhere near exhaustion!

We can experience the same in the spiritual realm. "I can't take one more trial and still hold on to Jesus." Or perhaps it takes too much effort to stay on track and dependently listen for His voice so that He can lay out His direction and will.

Many people who once were runners have given up. The self-discipline and time commitment required make it difficult to continue over the long haul. Similarly, many Christians who once desired a close, daily relationship with Jesus found that the self-discipline, effort, and time commitment were too much, so they gave up. Some leave the church, others resign themselves to a Christianity that is useful a few hours a week and then gets buried in the reality of daily life.

The devil doesn't seem to care how or why we give up our dependence on God, whether through laziness or lack of resolve in staying attached to Jesus. Alternatively, if he can get us to proceed independently to reach a certain goal, or if he can get us to push on in hopes that God will bless our plans that we are trying to accomplish, he is OK—as long as we are not depending on God. If we are self-reliant or dependent on anyone or anything other than Jesus, Satan's goal is accomplished.

Jesus wants the same unlimited trust and dependence from us that He demonstrated when He was on earth. Dependence is the only way to face the trials we encounter.

Consider how many times in the Bible we are referred to as sheep and Jesus as the Good Shepherd. Sheep? Couldn't we have been compared to something a little more desirable—perhaps a bear or a lion, maybe a cheetah or an eagle? But a sheep! Sheep are not terribly smart or awe-inspiring. They aren't very noble or gallant; they are just defenseless, relatively dumb animals that need their shepherd for guidance. This is precisely the point David was making when he wrote, "The Lord is my shepherd, I shall not want." The Lord is my defender, provider, knight in shining armor—because of this, I have need of nothing! Jesus can and will handle everything for me.

Jesus knew the Father would not allow the devil to do anything to change His earthly mission. Everything happened to Him for a reason. Every situation was planned by the Father and therefore a gift from Him to bring others to an understanding of God or to give glory to God. There was a reason behind everything that happened to Jesus.

In much the same way each situation that we encounter is for a purpose. It could be for my personal improvement or for the benefit of others and the glory of God if I respond in a spirit of true dependence. Thus, we can say with David, "The Lord is my shepherd, I shall not want." He has everything in control and provides everything that we need.

TRUSTING OTHER THINGS

The Bible warns about trusting or depending on things other than God. "Woe to those who go down to Egypt for help and rely on horses, who trust in chariots because they are many and in horsemen because they are very strong, but do not look to the Holy One of Israel or consult the Lord! . . . The Egyptians are men, and not God; and their horses are flesh, and not spirit" (Isa. 31:1-3, RSV).

"Your wisdom and your knowledge led you astray, and you said in your heart, 'I am, and there is no one besides me'" (Isa. 47:10, RSV).

"Cursed is the man who trusts [depends] in [on] man and makes flesh his arm, whose heart turns away from the Lord" (Jer.17:5, RSV).

Contemplate the story of God leading the Israelites out of slavery from Egypt. The journey to the Promised Land was more than just a matter of transporting a people across the desert into Canaan. If getting them to Canaan had been His sole purpose, God could have done it in a much more efficient way and along a much easier route. The desert journey was one of learning dependence on God.

As slaves, they had no means of freeing themselves from one of the most powerful nations of the time. They had no training in or knowledge of how to live in the harsh desert they were about to cross. They had no ability to furnish their own water, food, or garments. They needed shelter from the cold desert nights and shade from the searing daytime heat. Without divine intervention, there would never have been enough resources for several million people to survive such an extreme journey. It was imperative the Israelites learn dependence on God.

Moses reflects on Israel's experience:

"In a desert land he found him [Israel], in a barren and howling waste. He shielded him and cared for him; he guarded him as the apple of his eye, like an eagle that stirs up its nest and hovers over its young, that spreads its wings to catch them and carries them aloft. The Lord alone led him; no foreign god was with him. He made him ride on the heights of the land and fed him with the fruit of the fields. He nourished him with honey from the rock, and with oil from the flinty crag, with curds and milk from herd and flock and with fattened lambs and goats, with choice rams of Bashan and the finest kernels of wheat" (Deut. 32:10-14).

Our own journey from sin-slavery to our Promised Land parallels that of the Israelites' pilgrimage to Canaan. Is God's purpose any different? The Israelites had to put their dependence on God before they could leave Egypt. If they had remained dependent on the Egyptians or even Pharaoh, they would never have left on the long journey. But losing their submissive spirit would have meant forfeiting their Promised Land. Likewise, our dependence on Jesus is imperative to fully leaving our sin-slavery and embracing our Promised Land.

"Your salvation requires you to turn back to me and stop your silly effort to save yourselves. Your strength will come from settling down in complete dependence on me—The very thing you've been unwilling to do" (Isa. 30:15, Message).

CHAPTER 2

WHAT EXACTLY
IS DEPENDENCE?

At New Beginnings Ranch, a spiritual retreat center that my family and I manage, we learn about dependence through an activity involving rope-assisted rock climbing. The climbers must wear masks so that they cannot see the rock wall. Therefore, they have to depend on another person to give them specific instructions on how to proceed up the wall. "Move your right hand to the level of your shoulder—just a little farther up and out—yeah, that's it. Now move . . ." The climber must rely completely on information provided by the nonblindfolded assistant. It is often very hard for sighted climbers to be comfortable trusting something other than their own eyes.

Interestingly, the requirements for traversing the rock wall mirror biblical texts describing our dependence on God. The process involves four crucial steps:

1. Humbly understand that your need of help does not vary throughout the climb. Spiritually, you need a Savior every minute of your life.

2. Know and accept that your "sighted" guide can help you traverse the steep and potentially arduous climb. Likewise, know and accept Jesus as your sovereign Creator and Savior. Believe He is working things out for your good, even if you do not see how that could happen.

3. Submit to your seeing guide's instructions as you climb. We continually search for and submit to God's will, including any action or inaction that He allows.

4. Have continual two-way communication with your guide, which allows for accurate and safe traversing of the route. In our spiritual walk, continual two-way communication with God allows us to do His will in the moment, every moment.

Some individuals on the climbing route decide to proceed without their guide's instructions, ultimately leading to retracing steps as they pursue the final goal. At other times, poor communication slowed or halted progress.

Once, two sisters were involved in one of these "discipleship adventures." One was climbing blindfolded, receiving instructions from a ground spotter who gave detailed instructions. Halfway through the route, her sister, from the rocks above, began giving directions that were not as clear or detailed as the previous ones. Surprisingly, the climbing sister was able to progress faster along the route with the assistance of her nonblindfolded sister. The relationship of these sisters enhanced a clear understanding between them. The closer a relationship between two people, the more clear-cut the instructions can be delivered and received. In much the same way, as we grow closer to Jesus, learning to recognize and understand His voice, His instructions become clearer and more applicable.

In order for true dependence to work, all four of the requirements for blindfolded climbing must be met. In spite of the disciples' close relationship with Jesus, they still had trouble depending on God. Contrast their attitudes in the upper room on the night of Jesus' betrayal with how they responded at Pentecost. They all had a personal relationship with Jesus and frequent two-way communication with their Lord (part of the dependence picture). In the upper room they didn't realize they were inadequate in themselves and needed a Savior. They were all independently vying for the top position in the new kingdom they thought Jesus would set up. There was no submission of their wills when it came time to wash the feet of the group. Self-confident and self-reliant, they failed to recognize their need of help outside themselves.

Jesus had tried to show them true dependence throughout His ministry. He maintained communication with the Father, continually submitting to the Father's will, and showed that even without His heavenly powers it was possible to conquer the devil by maintaining dependence on the Father. The disciples came to understand this after the Resurrection, and their new dependence made a dramatic change in each of them. Humbly understanding the need of a Savior, accepting Jesus as the sovereign Savior, submitting to His will, and maintaining communication with heaven changed them radically. Pentecost was the result! From bumbling wimps who jumped at every noise after the Crucifixion, to boldly proclaiming the gospel in the face of torture and death, Jesus' disciples demonstrated the power of learning dependence. This same understanding in our lives will radically transform us into His likeness.

"Do not be conformed to this world but be transformed by the renewal of your mind" (Rom. 12:2, RSV). Transformation changes our independence to dependence.

Remember Jesus' admonition to ask, seek, and knock?

"To ask is to depend on someone other than yourself. It is very humbling. Asking indicates:

"I don't know."

"I failed."

"I ran out."

"I can't find it."

"I'm not sure."

"I don't understand."

"I forgot."

"I didn't listen."

"I didn't care."

"I was wrong."

"I need more information."

"I came up short."

"That's why Jesus said we should ask. Asking puts us back on track with God. It assumes a need relationship with him—a hand-to-mouth spiritual existence. A vulnerable daily dependence" ("True Believers Don't Ask Why," by John Fischer, in *NIV Men's Devotional Bible*, p. 1205. Copyright 1989 by John Fischer. Bethany House Publishers).

Seeking indicates that we recognize that while we do not have the answers, He does. It demonstrates that we trust enough to search for answers and truth in Him. Knocking signals our willingness to allow Him to take control of our lives. It also demonstrates our need of an intimate, dependent relationship with Him.

CHAPTER 3

PRIDE, IS IT A BIG DEAL?

In the next four chapters we will visit each of the four crucial items that make up dependence. The first of these elements is that of humility, our acceptance of our own need!

During my years of training in medical school, residency, and finally fellowship, I was often frustrated when others landed the best residency spots or fellowship jobs solely because of whom they knew. I believed that one should be accepted into programs based on academic achievements and hard work—not because of knowing important people. I wondered what they had done to deserve the better residency or fellowship. Graduating very high in my medical school class and scoring extremely well on my board exams should have gotten me a preferred spot, I reasoned. Some of these colleagues had been only in the middle of their medical school class and had quite average board scores. I scratched my head, wondering at the criteria by which these "inferiors" got the better jobs.

I never verbalized my thoughts, but I had, in fact, worked very hard to achieve my education, and felt consternation at seeing others who had "played around" during their training get as good or better spots than I. I was not more talented academically than most of my peers, but I thought I should be rewarded for my diligence. Personal accomplishment should have been the basis of the assignments instead of riding on the achievements of the person doing the recommending. I wanted to be recognized for *my* accomplishments, not someone else's.

Humility is the first and most important step in moving to a state of dependence with Jesus. It's not about me getting recognition for what I have done. It's not about my accomplishments or hard work. It's not about the struggles that I have gone through. It's not about getting the glory and prestige I deserve. It's about God's presence working through me and my giving all of the glory to Him. Unfortunately, it is one of the most difficult steps for us. As the above illustration shows, the Lord had a lot of work to do on my heart to develop humility. It is an ongoing work, as well!

"These are the ones I look on with favor: those who are humble and contrite in spirit" (Isa. 66:2). "He guides the humble in what is right and teaches them his way" (Ps. 25:9).

"I live . . . also with the one who is contrite and lowly in spirit, to revive the spirit of the lowly and to revive the heart of the contrite" (Isa. 57:15).

Those are powerful texts! "These are the ones I look on with favor"—hold high, value—"the one who is contrite and lowly in spirit" (such as the publican). "He guides the humble." "I live also with the one who is contrite and lowly in spirit." What more could we possibly want than to humbly be who He created us to be? What could be more important than to have Him guide and live with us?

C. S. Lewis states in *Mere Christianity* (p. 94), that pride is the "essential vice, the utmost evil. . . . It was through Pride that the devil became the devil: Pride leads to every other vice: it is the complete anti-God state of mind."

Since pride is the root and heart of sin since its inception, God is quite vocal about His feelings toward it.

"The fear of the Lord is hatred of evil. Pride and arrogance and the way of evil and perverted speech I hate" (Prov. 8:13, RSV).

"Haughty eyes and a proud heart—the unplowed field of the wicked—produce sin" (Prov. 21:4).

"God opposes the proud but shows favor to the humble" (James 4:6).

"Concerning the sinfulness of the wicked: There is no fear of God before their eyes. In their own eyes they flatter themselves too much to detect or hate their sin" (Ps. 36:1).

Pharisaical pride and arrogance blinded the leaders of Jesus' day to the foolishness of their reasoning. Failing to see their true spiritual condition, they received Christ's strongest condemnations. The parable of the Pharisee and the publican contrasts the spirit behind two ways of relating to God. The Pharisee was proud of his ability to do all the things he deemed important, working expectantly for increased favor. He was eager to tell God about his great track record, and he let out a sigh of relief because he outpaced the publican. Conversely, the publican recognized his complete inability to measure up. He came humbly seeking forgiveness and admitting his dependence on a God much bigger than himself.

True sincerity brings God to us, recognizing that "all that we have accomplished you have done for us" (Isa. 26:12).

We bring nothing, He offers everything. We acknowledge our desperate need of Him, He moves on our behalf. In an act of inexplicable resourcefulness, He exclaims, "My grace is sufficient for you, for my power is made perfect in weakness" (2 Cor. 12:9, RSV).

Dependence begins with a humble confession that we are personally incapable of directing our life journey. Although David was a very successful warrior before and after taking the throne, he was quick to give due credit for his triumphs.

"I put no trust in my bow, my sword does not bring me victory; but you give us victory over our enemies, you put our adversaries to shame. In God we make our boast all day long, and we will praise your name forever" (Ps. 44:6-8).

Notwithstanding David's extraordinary success, he was keenly aware of his true position before God. "I am poor and needy; may the Lord think of me. You are my help and my deliverer; you are my God, do not delay" (Ps. 40:17).

David had abundant wealth as king of Israel, yet he knew his success was God-generated and that he was as destitute as those over whom he ruled—"destitute" in the sense of his deep dependent need of God as his strength, fortress, refuge, shield, and deliverer. Perhaps this was the reason he was called a man after God's own heart.

Humility is an integral part of the dependent walk with God, albeit the most difficult. We want the praise and honor for our accomplishments— "After all, I did work pretty hard to get that good grade—or job promotion— or prestigious position." This is not what David is speaking of here. "In God we make our boast all day long, and we will praise your name forever" (Ps. 44:8). Our only boasting is in God, and we should praise His name for making our success possible.

When John fell at the feet of the angel, the angel said, "Do not worship me; worship God" (see Rev. 22:9).

Psalm 115:1 says: "Not to us, Lord, not to us but to your name be the glory." To see God's work in our lives, we must become humble, needy, and poor in spirit.

"He raises the poor from the dust and lifts the needy from the ash heap; he seats them with princes" (Ps. 113:7, 8).

"But he lifted the needy out of their affliction" (Ps. 107:41).

"For he stands at the right hand of the needy" (Ps.109:31).

We must have a need before God can fulfill it. Whether the need is spiritual, financial, emotional, relational, or physical, we are propelled to

Him through the very place of our desperation. Jesus illustrated this in the story of the rich young ruler (Mark 10). Asking for the young man's "all" revealed a spirit-deficiency he was unaware he harbored. Jesus wanted to meet him at the point of this need.

What precipitated Jesus' execution on the cross? Mark 3 reveals the plans of the Pharisees and Sadducees as they prepared to kill Jesus. It appears their pride, arrogance, and vested interest in preserving their traditions led them to crucify our Lord. Sadly, the same weaknesses in our characters could lead us to do the very same thing.

SELF-TRUST/-DISTRUST

Peter's experience in denying his Lord reveals a less-apparent aspect of humility.

"When Peter said he would follow his Lord to prison and to death, he meant it, every word of it; but he did not know himself. . . . The Savior saw in him a self-love and assurance that would overbear even his love for Christ. Much of infirmity, of unmortified sin, carelessness of spirit, unsanctified temper, heedlessness in entering into temptation, had been revealed in his experience. Christ's solemn warning was a call to heart searching. Peter needed to distrust himself, and to have a deeper faith in Christ. Had he in humility received the warning, he would have appealed to the Shepherd of the flock to keep His sheep. . . . But Peter felt that he was distrusted, and he thought it cruel. He was already offended, and he became more persistent in his self-confidence" (*The Desire of Ages,* pp. 673, 674).

In other words, Peter needed a healthy distrust of himself and his commitment to his Lord. His self-assurance and self-love needed to be changed into God-assurance and love. Self-distrust is a mandatory part of our first steps toward dependence on God. Satan will take advantage of any portion of our heart that hangs on to self-reliance, just as he did with Peter.

After Peter came to the terrible realization that he was capable of denying the very Christ he had pledged to follow to prison or death, he came face-to-face with the truth about himself. His self-assurance was gone. He no longer trusted his own abilities and realized how imperative it was to depend on God's strength. At this point, Jesus could enter his weakness and begin to work His power through Peter.

SUBMIT OR HOLD ON TO CONTROL

We are all faced, at varying times in our lives, with our inability to control the circumstances we experience, contrasted with the beauty of God's sovereignty. Do we respond in humble submission to God and His purposes or is there defiant independence and hardening of our hearts? In Exodus, Pharaoh exhibited a defiant response to his lack of control in light of God's providence. Each time he was faced with God's sovereign power he responded from a willful heart.

How are you responding to the situations in your life that you cannot control? Maybe there are health issues, a crumbling marriage, abuse, unemployment, or any number of smaller things you face on a daily basis. Will you respond in defiant independence or in humble acceptance asking, "Lord, what wilt thou have me to do?" (Acts 9:6, KJV).

Jesus admonished, "He who is least among you will be the greatest." The one who is least in their own eyes has the potential for the greatest dependence and thus to be greatest in God's eyes.

We will not move very far in our efforts to develop good marriages until we understand that repairing a damaged sense of identity and healing the wound in our hearts is not the first order of business. It is rather dealing with the subtle, pervasive, stubborn commitment to ourselves.

"Self-centeredness is the killer. In every bad relationship, it is the deadliest culprit. Poor communication, temper problems, unhealthy responses to dysfunctional family backgrounds, codependent relation-ships, and personal incompatibility—everything (unless medically caused) flows out of the cesspool of self-centeredness" ("Men and Women," by Lawrence Crabb, Jr., in NIV Men's Devotional Bible, p. 1351. Copyright 1991, Zondervan Publishing House).

"I am personally convinced that this submission, this dying to self, this crucifying of pride (Phil. 2:1-8) is crucial to our joy. We think of denying self as somber, grim-faced business when it is in truth a prelude to dancing. If you want power, learn to be assertive. If you want joy, learn to be submissive. . . . The reason our death (to self) increases the joy level all around is that it also increases the love level all around. Only when we die to self can we fully love one another. Self is a devilish creature, demanding all of our energy, wanting our constant attention, reaching even into our pocketbooks for favors. How can we be attuned to another's spirit when self is making so much noise? How can we ever hope to love another when self screams for our constant care? When self is alive and well, it offers us an all-or-nothing proposition. We either pacify self, or we crucify it" ("Dancing Into Zion," by Judson B. Edwards, in NIV Men's

Devotional Bible, p. 1215. Copyright 1986, Zondervan Publishing House).

Why aren't we successful in our evangelism, as the disciples were after Jesus went back to heaven? Perhaps we are living the lives the disciples led before the Crucifixion. Look at us, vying for the top position at work, the lead tenor in the choir; or the lead violin in the orchestra; the lead spiker on the volleyball team, or the primary shooting guard on the basketball team.

We *want* to be first.

We do not *want* to "wash the feet" of our fellow humans.

We do not *want* to listen implicitly to all directions from the Spirit. We do not *want* to put everything at stake personally for Jesus and His kingdom.

We do not *want* to humbly follow and submit.

Humility is only the first part of this first step. We need to humbly accept that we are in need of a *Savior*. We have nothing in ourselves that is worth saving (our righteousness is as filthy rags). We need Someone to pull us out of this pit of sin and degradation. We need forgiveness for the past and a Presence in the present, a Presence that can save us the regrets and despair of living outside of a life of dependence on Him. Face it, we need help!

The pride and selfishness trap turns up in many forms. It parades as control issues—not allowing God to be the pilot of my life, or perhaps craving control over others. Hypocrisy—trying to look good or hide my imperfections—is based in pride and selfishness. One of the more insidious types of pride is that of spiritual arrogance. "I am a better Christian than so and so because . . ." Pride in any form creates enmity between human and human and between humans and God.

Pride and arrogance are at the root of most of our interpersonal conflicts. We guard our rights and don't want to humbly admit our mistakes and ask forgiveness for wrongs done.

How do we step away from the pride and selfishness trap? I am slowly learning the necessity of basic self-distrust. The human heart is wicked, even when we are learning to be God's children. We can learn the way Peter did—experientially, or we can learn from others' mistakes—vicariously. Ask the Lord to point out where we may be harboring conceit and egocentricity. It takes a humble heart to allow God to reveal our deficiencies and a spiritual maturity to face those deficits. Following His revelation, the next step will vary by individual.

In my life, I need to consciously level the playing field around me.

Because I am a physician, others often treat me differently. I can sometimes believe in my heart this differing treatment is warranted and necessary. But the ground is level at the foot of the cross. So I encourage people to avoid using "Doctor" before my name except when I'm working in the hospital. (I was told by a devout Quaker that adherents of that faith do not use titles before their names, presumably to prevent arousing pride and selfishness.) When receiving a compliment on something that I did well, I acknowledge it as a blessing from God, recognizing Him as the source of my strength.

We must humbly admit—"all that we have accomplished You have done for us" (Isa. 26:12). When we see that we accomplish all things through Him alone—even our next breath or next step is achieved only through Him—our sense of humility is fostered and cultivated.

Sometimes giving God the glory is difficult for me when, after an arduous surgery, the patient does exceptionally well. Satan then tempts me by provoking pride in the job that "I did." However, vanity and self-exaltation cannot coexist in an atmosphere of humility, when I remember the Source of my power. Truly, my abilities come to me only through the mercy and grace of God.

Practicing humility is important in other areas, such as giving. It may be best to give anonymously so that the person contributing is not lifted up. Though recognition is a common means of encouraging the wealthy to donate, acknowledging the giver rather than the Giver behind the gift smacks of self-veneration.

"When you give to the needy, do not let your left hand know what your right hand is doing, so that your giving may be in secret. Then your Father, who sees what is done in secret, will reward you" (Matt. 6:3, 4).

Unfortunately, even Christians can feed this prideful independence in each other. When we praise the human vehicle for anything from a musical performance to a sermon well presented to a generous gift to the church, we miss an opportunity to lift up the Source of all talents. Focusing on the gift that has come through a human agent leads to human pride, and we lose the opportunity to reflect the glory back to God, the wellspring of all our accomplishments.

Jesus goes on in Matthew 6:7, 8 to warn against praying in the synagogues and on the street corners to be seen by others. Giving glory to anything or anyone other than God—even in prayer—brings condemnation!

Humility is understanding my limitations and insignificance without Jesus while realizing the limitless possibilities available to me in Him.

Neither leads me to boast or be puffed up. This is not a matter of self-degradation or self-deprecation. It is simply a realization of my sinfulness and weakness without Him in contrast to the offer of His righteousness and strength when I accept His invitation to submission.

Humility does not doubt my ability to accomplish the work given me by God. Moses, one of the most humble men in the Bible, was confronted at the burning bush with a very large job proposal. He responded by telling God that he was not capable of leading the Israelites. His response was not a result of humility but demonstrated a lack of confidence in God's judgment and His ability to accomplish His purpose. True humility is a willingness to do what God asks of me, in His timing, with a constant awareness that He is the one doing it. Humility involves taking my eyes off myself and focusing solely on Him. We work to glorify God in everything instead of taking any of the glory to ourselves.

It was said that the secret of Mother Teresa's life was that she was free (and willing) to be nothing. Therefore, God could use her for anything.

GOD IS HUMBLE?

The fact that God wanted all the glory actually bothered me quite a bit earlier in my life. What kind of God would be like that?

Matthew 11:28, 29 states: "Come to me, all you who are weary and burdened, and I will give you rest. Take my yoke upon you and learn from me, for I am gentle and humble in heart, and you will find rest for your souls."

Philippians 2:6-8: "Who, being in very nature God, did not consider equality with God something to be used to his own advantage; rather, he made himself nothing by taking the very nature of a servant, being made in human likeness. And being found in appearance as a man, he humbled himself by becoming obedient to death—even death on a cross."

Jesus was and is humble. He took on humanity (the biggest revelation of His humility) to show us the Father ("If you have seen Me, you have seen the Father"). Remember, He didn't come as a prince, but as the lowliest of paupers. He was born in a barn and during His ministry had no spot even to place His head. The Creator of the universe didn't just lower Himself to our level. He lowered Himself to that of the lowest in society. Humility!

Jesus is humble, and so is the Father. That being the case, why would He require all of Creation to acknowledge His sovereignty and give Him glory?

Max Lucado, in *Traveling Light*, page 74, reminds us that the struggle with humility is our problem, not God's. "Praise swells our heads and shrinks our brains, and pretty soon we start thinking we had something to do with our survival. Pretty soon we forget we were made out of dirt and rescued from sin."

There is perfect balance in and between each member of the Godhead. Praise does not change who They are. It does not lift Them up in Their own minds. They can receive praise without it "going to Their heads." All of Creation does not have the balance of the Godhead. Praise that is given to us *does* lift us up in our own eyes. Consider Lucifer, flawless at his creation, who was thrown down from the heights of heaven because he became filled with pride.

Giving God all praise protects us from self-exaltation and the resultant separation from Him that accompanies pride. It is a protection for us and ultimately for the universe. Selfishness and arrogance are at the very heart of sin, which destroyed the beauty of this world and cast a shadow on His universe. God rejoices when we ask Him to weed these things out of our lives. He wants to banish pride forever so that eternity can be filled only with His joy and salvation.

CHAPTER 4

IS ANYTHING TOO BIG FOR JESUS?

The second crucial element of dependence is recognizing Jesus as our Sovereign, Creator, and Savior. Thankfully we do have a Savior who has already come to be "Emmanuel," or "God is with us."

"For God so loved the world that he gave his one and only Son, that whoever believes in him shall not perish but have eternal life. For God did not send his Son into the world to condemn the world, but to save the world through him" (John 3:16, 17).

These verses can become so familiar that we miss their astounding significance. *We have a Savior!* Not only do we have a Savior, He is our Creator and He is God.

"In the beginning was the Word, and the Word was with God, and the Word was God. He was with God in the beginning. Through him all things were made; without him nothing was made that has been made. In him was life, and that life was the light of all mankind" (John 1:1-4).

As He is God, He has all the power and sovereignty, as has the rest of the Godhead. "I am the Lord, the God of all mankind. Is anything too hard for me?" (Jer. 32:27).

It is critical that we realize that Jesus is our Savior and that He is not only our Savior, but our *Sovereign* Savior. We could have someone else save us, but that being might not have the power to protect us and orient our lives in a way to accomplish an ultimate goal. Jesus is our Creator and Savior and is sovereign. He has the power and the will to work all circumstances for our good, even when it feels that He doesn't. "And we know that in all things God works for the good of those who love him, who have been called according to his purpose" (Rom. 8:28).

Accepting God's providence and our utter inability to control circumstances is where faith begins. Faith, or our belief system, allows us to depend fully on Jesus. Too often we attempt to bring God down to our level, putting Him in a box that we can understand, giving Him a form that is less abstract to us. Unfortunately, this effectively strips God of the very power He is exhibiting in our lives! We become our own god because we believe we have the answers to our life questions and circumstances—basically humanism in the guise of Christianity.

Isaiah understood his own insignificance when he encountered the power and majesty of God. "Woe is me! For I am lost; for I am a man of unclean lips, and I dwell in the midst of a people of unclean lips; for my eyes have seen the King, the Lord of hosts!" (Isa. 6:5, RSV). We desperately need such an encounter ourselves!

One Sabbath afternoon this understanding of *my* inadequacy and *His* sovereignty became apparent in a very tangible way. I was to go to a friend's house for Sabbath dinner one cloudy winter day, and I was hurrying a bit too fast. The thermometer hovered around the freezing mark as I left the hospital, changed clothes, and headed out. My route took me from dry pavement onto a gravel road hard-packed with snow. I wasn't particularly worried, as I had learned to drive in North Dakota—a good learning ground for winter driving! Coming up to a 90-degree left turn, I began to slow from about 40 miles per hour. The brakes engaged, but my vehicle started sliding with almost no deceleration. I turned the wheel and pumped the brakes, but there was absolutely no response to any of my efforts.

The road ended at a "T" intersection, and directly ahead was a canal filled with water. When I realized where I was headed, my worst fear came to mind—being in a vehicle trapped below the water's surface. I immediately cried out, "No, Lord!" I tried desperately to turn left and slow down but my vehicle continued sliding with the front pointing slightly to the left.

Just after I sent up my urgent prayer, I struck a pile of dirt with the right front end of my van, turning the van and thus my direction of travel almost completely to the left, where there was a bridge. Slowing just slightly, I hit the edge of the bridge with my left front tire and gradually slid down the side of the bridge, gently landing on the ice at the edge of the canal. There I sat, perched precariously, with the van's right front end sitting on the ice only a few feet from the running water of the canal. Only a plastic bumper—and a prayer—held up the rear end of the van!

Stunned, I sat a minute, wondering if I was injured. Realizing that I didn't have a scratch or even a bruise, I turned off the engine, unlatched my seat belt, and jumped out of the vehicle. I pulled myself onto the side of the bridge, up and away from the wreckage. Breathing a prayer of thankfulness and praise, I called a tow truck.

When the wrecker pulled my van up the bank, the ice that had been supporting the front of my vehicle broke away and floated down the canal. The water was estimated to be about 10 feet deep at that point. Just a little more momentum . . . or a little more weight in the vehicle (my wife and children had intended to join me that weekend but canceled their plans at the last minute) . . . or the front left tire not slowing my speed on the edge of the bridge, and likely I would have gone through the ice.

Did this catch my attention? You bet it did! I had been saved from my worst nightmare and left it without a scratch, bruise, or even getting wet. All I could do was humbly drop to my knees and say, "Thank You, Lord. What do You have in mind for my life?"

Moses experienced the fear of God when God showed him His glory (Ex. 33:18-23). Peter, James, and John experienced the same awe on the Mount during Jesus' transfiguration (Matt. 17:1-8). The fear of God puts us in our rightful place. We understand that we are a speck in the universal plan, but somehow, are still important to the Almighty. Proverbs 9:10 states, "The fear of the Lord is the beginning of wisdom." It is the beginning of wisdom and dependence.

The Old Testament echoes the recurring theme of God's discipline of the Hebrew people. Why? First, they had forsaken God, and second, they were worshipping other gods—the creation of their own hands (Jer. 1:16; Jer. 2:13). In other words, they were elevating themselves and dethroning God.

If you cannot depend on Him, why? Is your God so small it makes trusting Him difficult? Do you feel so self-sufficient that you don't need His help? If you really understand how great He is and how much He desires to help, coupled with a realization of your own desperate need, dependence will be a natural response. At this point, He enters and begins *His* work. "My power is made perfect in weakness" (2 Cor. 12:9).

CHAPTER 5

ARE YOU WILLING
TO SUBMIT TO HIM?

We may humbly understand that we need help and cannot do life on our own. We may understand that Christ is our Creator and came to save us. We may even understand what God wants us to do in the moment, but without submission of the will to His, we will have none of the power of a dependent relationship with Jesus.

If we know God but refuse to follow His direction in our lives, there is really no point in even knowing Him. "Do not be stiff-necked, as your ancestors were; submit to the Lord" (2 Chron. 30:8).

"But my people would not listen to me; Israel would not submit to me. So I gave them over to their stubborn hearts to follow their own devices. If my people would only listen to me, if Israel would only follow my ways, how quickly I would subdue their enemies and turn my hand against their foes!" (Ps. 81:11-14).

The next key in living the dependent life is full submission of our will to His. How can Jesus bless our lives and "subdue our enemies" without our faithful submission to His will?

Cesar Millan, a very successful dog trainer/rehabilitator, believes that a dog's owner must lead their dog much as a pack leader would lead other dogs. The only way to have a well-behaved, balanced dog is to have a calm, submitted dog. Dogs do not behave well when they are in control. They want to have someone in charge, someone who looks out for their best interest, who protects and provides for them. When the dog is in control, behavioral issues such as stress, aggression, and fear surface. The dog becomes the pack leader instead of a calm, submitted follower.

We need to have a calm, submitted attitude toward our Leader. We don't have to live with the stress, aggression, and fear that result from trying to be in control. We have Someone willing and eager to provide support and care. We can live a life of joy in a calm, submitted state, depending on the true Pack Leader.

The same weekend I slid into the canal a friend of mine died. He was about my age, a dedicated disciple of Christ, who went out of his way to make others feel comfortable in his presence as well as in His presence. Why was his outcome different from mine that weekend? My wife sagely reminded me that she would have had to accept God's answer, regardless of what it was, just as my friend's wife did.

We do not know the "why" of many of our life experiences. We can find comfort and strength in submitting to an all-knowing and all-powerful God who loves us and wants the best for us in the midst of our sinful environment. Unfortunately, we have a tough time trusting God fully, especially when things don't make sense. Submission becomes a difficult step into the unknown.

During a trip I made to Haiti after the earthquake of 2010, which I will describe in more detail later, we encountered incredible fear in every patient we brought into the operating room. Each one panicked at the thought that we might have to do an amputation. Even if we were treating a closed fracture (one with the skin intact over the bones) or something relatively minor, the patients were terrified we were going to amputate some part of their body.

This anxiety was so great in one patient with an open tibia fracture (broken shinbone sticking through the skin) that he refused to have his fracture cleaned in order to prevent an infection. We tried to tell him what we were going to do and that without this procedure he would most likely end up with what he feared most—an amputation. He just did not have enough confidence in us to allow us to do what needed to be done. After several days he returned, finally able to trust us. We did the surgery necessary to clean the exposed fracture, and later moved tissue over the break. When I left, it appeared that his leg would be saved.

Like my patient in Haiti, sometimes we have a hard time submitting our will to God's, even if it is the right thing. We can know rationally that it is best to trust and submit to Him, but we may be afraid. Fearing we are going to miss out on something we want to be part of, we leave a state of submission and put ourselves back in charge. Frequently, we are terrified that something will happen that we don't like—for example, losing a spouse. Ezekiel received an assignment by God that foretold he would lose his wife the next day. Situations like this strike at the core of our security and trust.

"Sacrifice is not giving up things, but giving to God with joy the best we have. . . . To go out in surrender to God means the surrendering of the miserable sense of my own unimportance; am I willing to surrender that mean little sense for the great big idea God has for me? Am I willing to surrender the fact that I am an ignorant, useless, worthless, too-old person? There is more hindrance to God's work because people cling to a sense of unworthiness than because of conceit. 'Who am I?' Instantly the trend of the mind is to say—'Oh well, I have not had any education'; 'I did not begin soon enough.' Am I willing to surrender the whole thing, and go out in surrender to God? To go out of the carnal mind into the spiritual—'fools for Christ's sake' (see 1 Corinthians 4:10)?" ("Daily Thoughts for Disciples," by Oswald Chambers, in *NIV Men's Devotional Bible,* p. 21. Copyright 1990, Discovery House Publishers).

We may believe superficially that God has our best interest in mind. But as Del Tackett inquires in the *Truth Project*, "Do you really believe that what you believe is really real?" Is there a disconnect between what you believe and what you *say* you believe? Are you really willing to fully depend on Jesus and submit to His purpose in your life?

"Submit yourselves, then, to God. Resist the devil, and he will flee from you. Come near to God and he will draw near to you" (James 4:7, 8).

CHAPTER 6

CAN WE REALLY EXPECT TO HEAR HIS VOICE?

In a dependent relationship one must *know* God's desires in order to humbly submit to those desires. Continual one-to-one communication is a necessity. Thankfully, God communicates with us in a variety of ways—through His Word, nature, providential circumstances, other godly people, our conscience, direct impressions, and a still small voice in our conscience. The difficult part can be discerning what is the voice of God from what isn't. The Bible, nature, and providential circumstances are fairly definitive in their origin, but when it comes to His other methods of communication it takes a lot of practice to truly discern whether something is from Jesus or whether it is from our self.

God has promised we can be in constant communion with Him just as Enoch was, and we can have the promptings of the Spirit to direct our footsteps. Look at these promises:

- "And your ears shall hear a word behind you, saying, 'This is the way, walk in it,' when you turn to the right or when you turn to the left" (Isa. 30:21, RSV).
- "I will instruct you and teach you the way you should go; I will counsel you with my eye upon you" (Ps. 32:8, RSV).
- "'They shall all be taught by God.' Every one who has heard and learned from the Father comes to me" (John 6:45, RSV).
- "Trust in the Lord with all your heart, and lean not on your own understanding; in all your ways acknowledge Him, and He shall direct your paths" (Prov. 3:5, 6, NKJV).
- "We are the temple of the living God. As God has said: 'I will live with them and walk among them, and I will be their God, and they will be my people.'" (2 Cor. 6:16).

When I speak about this concept of God directly communicating with us, some people become uncomfortable. They have so many thoughts going around in their minds they cannot tell which ones may or may not be from God. They are afraid that they may mistake their own selfish desires for the voice of God. Some are concerned that others will think they are "hearing voices" and conclude they're really delusional, possibly bordering on schizophrenia.

Whenever God has given us a special blessing, the devil has endeavored to make a counterfeit of it, even going so far as to make it a curse. For instance, consider God's gift of marriage and the devil's counterfeit of cohabiting without the benefit of marital commitment. Another example is the alternative theory of evolution, substituting for the beautiful story of Creation by a Creator-God who designed us in His image and loves us deeply.

The close relationship Jesus wants to have with us is no different. The devil wants to interfere and confuse our thoughts so that we question our ability to have the one-to-one communication so vital to spiritual survival and overall happiness. Satan wants us to think that: (1) God does not want to be closely involved with our lives; (2) it is impossible to discern the voice of God; and (3) those who think they can hear the voice of God must be emotionally unbalanced.

Let's go back to Elijah and remember what the voice of God is like.

"And, behold, the Lord passed by, and a great and strong wind rent the mountains, and brake in pieces the rocks before the Lord; but the Lord was not in the wind: and after the wind an earthquake; but the Lord was not in the earthquake: and after the earthquake a fire; but the Lord was not in the fire: and after the fire a still small voice" (1 Kings 19:11, 12, KJV).

God speaks to each of us in a still, small voice. His voice can be easily lost in the busyness of our lives, distractions around us, or even covered with our selfish wishes.

It is not difficult for the devil to mask that still small voice. He jams the airwaves of our minds by placing worries, impure thoughts, or simply nonsense to block God's communication. If those measures don't work, the devil can always go back to the old standby—inserting selfish thoughts and dreams. God does not usually make His voice heard above all the rest. If we desire to hear Him, we need to ask Him to eliminate or quiet the other voices so we can discern Him above the clamor. The devil, on the other hand, has no problem with compulsion or heavy-handedness toward us and our thoughts. He forces his ideas in a way that covers God's still small voice, often stirring us up—producing emotions that are not in line with Christ's government.

How can we discern God's voice from all the others? First and foremost, we must always test the impressions we have with Scripture. "Consult God's instruction and the testimony of warning. If anyone does not speak according to this word, they have no light of dawn" (Isa. 8:20).

"By this you know the Spirit of God: every spirit which confesses that Jesus Christ has come in the flesh is of God, and every spirit which does not confess Jesus is not of God" (1 John 4:2, 3, RSV).

In other words, if the impression honors Christ, accepts His sovereignty in our life, and leads us to do things that are in line with His law of love toward Him and others, it is likely from God's Spirit.

"Where the Spirit of the Lord is, there is freedom" (2 Cor. 3:17, RSV). The devil and self have a way of making their agenda a pushy, compulsive type of agenda. We know that this is not from God, as He stands for freedom and not compulsion. As noted above in 1 Kings 19:12, His is a still small voice.

If we want to be fully dependent on Jesus, we will need to hear and discern the voice of God. Three times in the book of Hebrews the same command is repeated. As there was no punctuation in the original manuscripts, repeating a thought gave it more importance. Repeating a thought three times gave a significant amount of importance to it. "Today, if you hear his voice, do not harden your hearts as you did in the rebellion" (Heb. 3:7, 8. See also verse 15 and Heb. 4:7).

Today, not tomorrow or sometime in the future; today you *will* hear Him. The Revised Standard Version (RSV) translates the passage as "*when* you hear his voice," but other translations state it as "*if* you hear His voice." I prefer to believe that God will talk to us today and every day, so I like the RSV. "Today, *when* (not if) you hear his voice, do not harden your hearts as in the rebellion." Listen and submit to His will for you right now. He *will* speak to you.

If you are willing to listen and respond to Him, He will continue to guide your footsteps. "They shall all be taught by God" (John 6:45, RSV).

My wife and daughters love horses. Most warm days in the winter and about five times a week in the summer, they can be found riding their horses. They don't just trail ride with the horses, they train them to do advanced maneuvers. To accomplish this difficult task, there must be interaction between the horse and its rider.

Recently my wife was excited to get our 63-inch horse to keep his front feet outside of a square made of timbers while keeping the back feet inside.

She communicated to this horse how to move his feet all the way around the square without touching the boards at any point. "Move to the side, then pivot around the corner, move to the side and pivot around the corner again." She worked patiently, communicating with her legs how he was to move. It took some fairly complex communication to maneuver a large animal so precisely. Four requirements had to be met:

- An experienced trainer.
- Years of training with the horse so that the horse knew what the rider was saying.
- A horse and rider that have worked together extensively.
- A calm, submissive, listening attitude on the part of the horse.

For God to maneuver us optimally within His will, we need the same components. Years of training our ears to listen, discerning what God is telling us and experiencing the problems that occur when we choose not to listen, show us how imperative it is to be in touch with Him. As we enter the relationship and listen with a humble, calm, submissive attitude, we learn to function within His will and follow Him completely.

God spoke to the backslidden people of ancient Israel as well as to us today in Psalm 81:11-13 (RSV):

"But my people did not listen to my voice; Israel would have none of me. So I gave them over to their stubborn hearts, to follow their own counsels. O that my people would listen to me, that Israel would walk in my ways!"

Did you hear the pathos of God? "O that my people would listen to me." Instead of being attentive to God, they followed the counsels of their stubborn hearts. With their minds set on what they wanted to happen, they willfully disobeyed even when the Lord showed them His way.

The inability (or unwillingness) to listen and submit to God's decree is displayed in the contrasting responses of Zechariah and Mary during their visits from the angel Gabriel. Zechariah and Elizabeth, you recall, were advanced in years and had no children. Gabriel visited Zechariah during his priestly obligations in the Temple, telling him, "Your prayer has been heard. Your wife Elizabeth will bear you a son, and you are to call him John" (Luke 1:13). Gabriel explains that John will not be an average child but will "make ready a people prepared for the Lord" (verse 17).

Zechariah responds: "How can I be sure of this? I am an old man, and my wife is well along in years" (verse 18).

This is a *priest* questioning Gabriel! Hey, Zechariah, don't you remember

Abraham and Sarah? Is your God too small to accomplish this? Are you listening to God, or are you living in the realm of visible human limitations?

Elizabeth became pregnant, and Zechariah got his tongue silenced until John's birth because of his unbelief and distrust.

Then there was Mary. Gabriel appeared to her and described her conception and the birth of her Son, Jesus. She did ask how this would happen, since she did not yet have a husband. Gabriel explained, "The Holy Spirit will come on you, and the power of the Most High will overshadow you. So the holy one to be born will be called the Son of God. . . . For no word from God will ever fail" (verses 35-37).

"'I am the Lord's servant,' Mary answered. 'May your word to me be fulfilled'" (verse 38). What a stark contrast between the two responses to Gabriel! Mary, in humble dependence, listened and submitted to God's will, even though it seemed pretty far-fetched. She *knew* the voice of God and really believed what she heard.

LACK OF COMMUNICATION WITH GOD

Why do we not hear God's voice on a regular basis? We have the promise "You will seek me and find me; when you search for me with all your heart" (Jer. 29:13, RSV).

What does it look like to seek and search for God with all your heart? If you sit down and read the Bible or a spiritually centered book for 15 or 20 minutes before going to bed, is that searching with all of your heart? Perhaps it would be more advantageous to spend time connecting with Him first thing in the morning. Then throughout the day, turn your thoughts and heart toward Him as you make decisions, interact with others, and ask His guidance in every situation you encounter. Could this be seeking and searching with all your heart? Can we expect to hear and commune with God when we are not feeding our relationship with Him? Do our self-decided priorities and plans crowd out the Savior? Jesus tells us in John 8:47: "Whoever belongs to God hears what God says. The reason you do not hear is that you do not belong to God."

In Isaiah 30:1 God describes the children of Israel thus: "'Woe to the obstinate children,' declares the Lord, 'to those who carry out plans that are not mine, . . . heaping sin upon sin.'" If we fail to walk in even the small amount of light that God has already given, will we be given more?

We are also told: "If I had cherished sin in my heart, the Lord would not have listened" (Ps. 66:18).

At one time my drive to work took me past a "gentleman's club" with a billboard outside that described upcoming events in sexually explicit terms. (I thought that no true gentleman would actually attend or read the billboard, but that was beside the point!) The messages on the sign did not keep my mind focused toward Christ. Each morning I had the choice to look at the billboard or look away. If I listened to the Holy Spirit, responding with my will in His favor, and accepting His power to deal with this temptation, I would progress through my day with Him and continue to hear His voice. (Thankfully, He has and continues to give me victory over that temptation.) If I trip on that temptation or any other along the way, I separate myself from God, and with my heart not in tune with Him I do not hear Him. As soon as I realize that I have separated myself from Him, I stop, ask His forgiveness and reconciliation, then I resurrender my thoughts, emotions, and life to Him. Back in relationship, I can again hear His voice directing my day. Throughout my life—and perhaps in yours—I can get tripped up early in the day and then choose not to put my hand back in God's, losing the remarkable connection God had planned for the day.

Being attuned to God's voice can dramatically affect the flow of our life during the course of a day. As a trauma orthopod, I have patients in the hospital who occasionally need prompt medical attention. On more than one occasion God has impressed me to begin visiting my patients on floors differently than is my usual routine. Often when I arrived to see a patient I would not normally have seen until later in the day, that patient needed attention right then. Coincidence? I choose not to think so.

One afternoon I was called to see a certain patient at the request of another physician. When the call came through, I was in surgery, so an OR (operating room) nurse answered, recording the message of where to go and why I was to see the patient. As there were two hospitals in this particular system, there was always a notation of "east" or "west" attached to the message to correctly identify the campus. After finishing surgery, and assured my patient was doing well, I picked up the message and went to the east campus, fourth floor to see the new patient.

Approaching the nurses' station, I noticed one of my surgical patients whom I had visited on rounds earlier that day. I felt impressed to check in on her to say hello. She had terminal cancer that had already spread to her bones. The cancer had weakened her femur (thighbone) and it had broken. I had operated on it so that she would not have severe, ongoing pain, which might even hasten her demise.

As I entered her room it was evident that something was wrong. She could barely catch her breath and had a hard time talking between rapid respirations. I quickly listened to her lungs and ordered some appropriate interventions. Sitting beside her, I took her hand in mine and calmly talked with her, easing her fears. With the interventions and the arrival of her medical doctor, she calmed down and began breathing normally.

Returning to the nurses' station, I asked about the patient I was to evaluate. "We didn't call you to check on anyone here," I was told. Puzzled, I stopped and pulled out the note from the operating-room nurse: "West campus, 4th floor." I was supposed to be on the fourth floor of *west* campus, not east! God directed me to the wrong campus so that I could stop in and see this patient who desperately needed intervention.

It is so important to hear and recognize God's voice as we experience countless decisions, frustrations, irritations, and temptations every day. We need God's direction to deal with life in a manner that honors Him.

Interruptions are very frustrating to me. When I am in the middle of something and my beeper or phone goes off, I feel annoyed. Sometimes I might be at a critical step of a surgery, or even struggling with a particular procedure; other times I may already have a long list of things to do and don't want to be bothered with yet another request. If my connection with Jesus is weak or nonfunctioning, I can become downright nasty!

Jesus' life was not always calm, slow, and nonirritating. I imagine He was pushed and pulled from all directions. On one hand, He was answering the questions of the Pharisees and Sadducees who were incessantly trying to double-cross Him. On the other hand, there were masses of sick people that crowded around Him for healing. The disciples were often bickering about who was the greatest and what rank they coveted in the upcoming kingdom. Sometimes they even sent children away from Jesus, claiming He was too busy. All these stressors, heaped upon Him, came on the heels of all-night prayer vigils that must have left Him sleep-deprived.

How did He deal with all of this? I could not have tolerated such stress. Jesus stated:

"The words I say to you I do not speak on my own authority. Rather, it is the Father, living in me, who is doing his work" (John 14:10).

"I do nothing on my own but speak just what the Father has taught me" (John 8:28). "For I did not speak on my own, but the Father who sent me commanded me to say all that I have spoken. I know that his command leads to eternal life. So whatever I say is just what the Father has told me to say" (John 12:49, 50).

Those all-night prayer vigils—they were essential to Jesus' dependence on His Father. Can we really have the same connection? "I tell you, whoever believes in me will do the works I have been doing, and they will do even greater things than these" (John 14:12). Can we expect to be able to stand against the devil without the connection that Jesus had with the Father?

In summary, (1) we must humbly accept that on our own, regardless of our efforts, we have nothing to offer that is worthy of salvation. (2) We need Someone to cover our past and change us completely so that we have hope, both in the present and the future. We must never lose sight of our desperate need every moment of every day. Jesus is not only our Savior, but our *sovereign* Savior. Even if we could have someone else save us, that being might not have the power to protect us and orient our lives in just the right way. Jesus is our Creator and Savior and He is sovereign—He has the power to work all circumstances for our good, even when it feels otherwise. (3) To have His power, we must continually submit our will to His. To submit to His purpose for our lives we must be (4) cognizant of His voice, making active communication with Him essential. Many times we have elements of this, but without all four, we are not truly depending on Him.

Is dependence inactivity, waiting for God to do everything for me at a later date? No, true dependence is demonstrated by someone like Abraham, who acted in response to God's instruction to leave his home for a foreign land. He also demonstrated the active nature of dependence when he followed God's instruction to take Isaac to Mount Moriah as a sacrifice.

When the Hebrews were at the edge of the Red Sea, "The Lord said to Moses, 'Why are you crying out to me? Tell the Israelites to move on'" (Ex. 14:15). God is not looking for inactivity. He is looking for our action in accordance with His will, in His timing.

CHAPTER 7

WHY DO WE NEED TO BE DEPENDENT?

CHILDLIKE DEPENDENCE

In Matthew 18:3 Jesus addresses the disciples' question of who is the greatest in the kingdom of heaven. "Truly I tell you, unless you change and become like little children, you will never enter the kingdom of heaven."

It was evening and I was home from work, playfully teasing my 2-and-a-half-year-old daughter. She had asked me once to quit playing with her hair. Several minutes later I again briefly ruffled her hair, and she again asked me to stop. I didn't bother her for several minutes, but couldn't resist pestering her one more time. Immediately she dropped to her knees and prayed, "Jesus, Daddy messin' my hair." Even at the tender age of 2 she knew where to go for help!

This is what Jesus is getting at: we need the pure, humble, transparent trust and dependence of a child or we will never enter the kingdom of heaven.

OTHER BIBLICAL REFERENCES TO DEPENDENCE

The Bible is full of illustrations of how God wants us to depend on Him. I will list only a few, barely skimming the surface of the multitudinous references.

In John 15:4-8 Jesus describes the complete dependence between branches and the vine.

"Remain in me, as I also remain in you. No branch can bear fruit by itself; it must remain in the vine. Neither can you bear fruit unless you remain in me. . . . Apart from me you can do nothing."

The week before His crucifixion, after talking to the scribes and Pharisees, Jesus stopped to mourn over the city. "Jerusalem, Jerusalem, you who kill the prophets and stone those sent to you, how often I have longed to gather your children together, as a hen gathers her chicks under her wings, and you were not willing" (Matt. 23:37, TNIV).

God's heart yearns to protect and care for us in the same way. He wants us to come to Him the way a dependent chick does to the mother hen.

"I have been crucified with Christ and I no longer live, but Christ lives in me. The life I now live in the body, I live by faith in the Son of God" (Gal. 2:20). What is being crucified with Christ? The independent, prideful, selfish part of a person before putting Christ on the throne of his or her life. After the independent self is crucified with Christ the individual lives in a surrendered life through dependence on Him.

The psalms of David contain an amazing number of references to dependence. David, the king of Israel, describes his complete dependence on God with imagery such as "refuge for the oppressed" (Ps. 9:9), "hide me in the shadow of your wings" (Ps. 17:8), "my strength," "my rock, my fortress and my deliverer," my "refuge, my shield and the horn of my salvation, my stronghold" (Ps. 18:2), "stronghold of my life" (Ps. 27:1), "he will keep me safe in his dwelling; he will hide me in the shelter of his sacred tent" (verse 5), "my strength and my shield" (Ps. 28:7), "The salvation of the righteous comes from the Lord; he is their stronghold in time of trouble. . . . He delivers them . . . and saves them, because they take refuge in him" (Ps. 37:39, 40). "My soul finds rest in God; my salvation comes from him. Truly he is my rock and my salvation; he is my fortress, I will never be shaken" (Ps. 62:1, 2).

What imagery is presented by the psalmist! What more could we ask for than what God is offering?

Consider the Jewish economy. The Israelites were asked to return 10 percent of their income to God. Then they were to give money to the Temple, provide sacrifices at feasts and when they committed sins, and give money to the poor. Every seven years they were to leave their fields fallow, and every 50 years they were to give all borrowed lands back to the original owners. This fiftieth year they were not to plant in their fields. Thus, food from the harvest of the forty-eighth year was to last until the harvest of the fifty-first year (the forty-ninth year farmland left fallow from the seven-year command and then the fiftieth from the year of jubilee command). There was no way for the Hebrews to make it on their own with this schedule of giving and not planting. This was exactly the point. God was their provider and He wanted them to remember this without a doubt. Without Him and His providence for them they would not survive, but with Him they were blessed beyond all others.

FOUR-WHEEL-DRIVE CHRISTIANITY

I arrived in Port-au-Prince, Haiti, nine days after the January 2010 earthquake that killed hundreds of thousands, injured countless others, and decimated the limited infrastructure. The medical needs of the injured were overwhelming. When I reached the hospital, patients with open fractures (bone penetrating the skin) were still finding their way to the operating room for initial treatment. (Can you imagine having an open fracture for nine days after a devastating earthquake?) Femur (thighbone) fractures were just starting to be addressed. On the medical level the needs were massive. The patients had no place to go after being treated, as their homes had been destroyed. There was a lack of food. Drinking water was in limited supply. Grief was pandemic, as nearly every person had lost family or close friends.

The day after my arrival a warning went out about the likelihood of another earthquake of equal or greater intensity than the first. The hospital needed to be evacuated for the safety of the patients and the relief workers. Many of the nurses and other helpers decided that to stay was too risky, so they took the next available flight out of the country. In the operating room I led in a short devotional with my staff, reminding them that God is in the business of growing our dependence on Him. *He* was the reason each of us had come to Haiti to help, and He was in control of the outcome of whatever transpired. While I couldn't guarantee we would be safe, we were assured He was ultimately in control. We didn't need to worry.

As we continued working, hospital resources began to improve, with the exception of one glaring deficiency—we had no transfusible blood. One particular surgery to stabilize a femur fracture took longer than expected, with more blood loss than usual. Although I was not part of the initial procedure, I became involved when the patient was brought back to the operating room later in the day for resuscitation. He *had* to have blood—and now! We did everything possible to acquire some blood from surrounding institutions, without success. Although we kept the patient alive for several hours, without the needed blood he eventually died.

The next day a patient returned to the operating room for a wound cleaning. The attending surgeons felt they had adequately cleaned the injury, but blood continued to ooze from the open wound. A tourniquet was placed to temporarily stem the flow until transfusible blood could be procured. Even though we were assured that blood would be available, none was forthcoming. The tourniquet had to be left in place to save his life, but in the process, the limb viability was lost.

I was devastated. A death from a preventable cause one night followed by an arm amputation from another preventable cause the next day was just too much. Although I hadn't been involved in either surgery and the amputated arm would have had a likelihood of poor function, this was still not the way it should go. I was trained to save lives and protect injured extremities. Preventable deaths and amputations were so unnecessary. I couldn't take it anymore. The weight of the needs was too great, and I was overwhelmed with the despair of failure. I was going home.

At this point God reminded me that it was true—*I* couldn't make a difference. Only *He* could make that difference if I allowed Him to work through me. When things didn't work out the way that I had planned, prayed, or wanted, the results were not in my hands, but His. After I had done my best through His strength and prayed for His blessing, if things didn't meet my expectations I had to step back and let Him be God.

It's often difficult for us to let things progress any other way than what we have in mind. We desperately want to be in control of circumstances until we realize we are in over our head, and then we ask God to take over. Sometimes, however, we still retain the "right" to decide the outcome instead of submitting to His will for the situation. When we're in trouble, we ask God to have control; otherwise, we feel we can handle it pretty well on our own.

I think of this as the "four-wheel-drive phenomenon." When I'm in my pickup I can choose two-wheel or four-wheel drive. Most of the time I drive my pickup in two-wheel drive, as it doesn't take as much gasoline to operate. The pickup is easier to handle in turns while in two-wheel drive, and it's easier on my tires. When I get into icy or very muddy conditions, I can easily turn a knob and go directly into four-wheel drive, enabling me to navigate deep snowdrifts or even glare ice with extra traction to keep going. When I am through the tough circumstances I can again turn the knob and return to two-wheel drive for better gas mileage, less wear on the tires, and easier turning.

Often this is how we relate to God. We want Him near to depend on when we are in conditions that require extra traction. But sometimes it takes too much energy to remain tightly connected with Him after we're through the tough circumstances. The dedication and effort to maintain a constant connection with Him may feel unnecessary for the daily encounters. Sometimes we need to make a quick decision and don't feel the need to wait for His leading. So, like with my pickup, we shift back into two-wheel drive (a self-directed life) in which we can be in charge and save some energy. After all, as long as He can be relied on to get us through the rough spots maybe we don't really need Him for the small stuff.

Our heavenly Example didn't say that the important things that I do and say are from the Father. He said, "The words I say to you I do not speak on my own authority. Rather, it is the Father, living in me, who is doing his work" (John 14:10). Jesus also said that without Me you can do nothing. Nothing is pretty exclusive, even the "small stuff."

HUNGERING AND THIRSTING?

"Blessed are they who hunger and thirst for righteousness, for they shall be filled" (Matt. 5:6, NKJV). Many of us are hungering and thirsting, but never find the spot where we are filled. We try to get filled with more money, more things, more prestige, more power, better grades, prettier clothes, or more understanding or more luring to significant others; better travel destinations, and on and on. We want more—and better.

If we are thirsting for a million dollars, will we be satisfied if somehow we get it? Of course not; we would need even more to be gratified. If we are pursuing a more alluring "significant other" and are able to win their attention and affection, are we satisfied? Short-term satisfaction, perhaps, until a more appealing individual of the opposite sex comes along and we are off again, trying to win their affections.

We attempt to drink at fountains that do not satisfy or fulfill. Whatever we chase or depend on for our identity outside of Jesus will require more and more grasping, ending—sadly—without much satisfaction past the present moment. This is why Jesus asks us to surrender any other ventures and make them subservient to our relationship with Him. The rich young ruler was asked to give up his dependence on riches so that he could have the more abundant life Jesus offered.

"Let anyone who is thirsty come to me and drink" (John 7:37).

"Admission of thirst doesn't come easy for us. False fountains pacify our craving with sugary swallows of pleasure. But there comes a time when pleasure doesn't satisfy. There comes a dark hour in every life when the world caves in and we are left trapped in the rubble of reality, parched and dying.

"Some would rather die than admit it . . . 'God, I need help.'

"So the thirsty come. A ragged lot we are, bound together by broken dreams and collapsed promises. Fortunes that were never made. Families that were never built. Promises that were never kept. . . .

"And we are very thirsty. Not thirsty for fame, possessions, passion or romance. We've drunk from those pools. They are salt water in the desert. They don't quench—they kill" ("The Applause of Heaven," by Max Lucado, in *NIV Men's Devotional Bible*, p. 1138. Copyright 1990, Word Inc., Dallas, Texas).

It's often difficult not to chase after and cling to our independence and the direction we'd like for our lives. Earlier in my career as a trauma orthopod, I wanted to be recognized as an expert, not just locally but nationally. I worked hard, taking care of difficult fractures and studying the best methods of care for those difficult fractures. I presented research at meetings, published papers, and even wrote part of a chapter in the *Orthopedic Knowledge Update: Trauma 3*. Was it enough? No, I had to do more and publish more so that I could maintain the recognition I had and also to gain further recognition.

I was still going to church, studying my Bible and praying almost every day, occasionally praying with the patients I operated on. Doing many of the right things and many times for the right reasons, I still was not depending on God for my daily direction and ultimate destiny. I was using Him only for the four-wheel-drive capability that He gave me.

Thankfully, He came through for me even when I was using Him for His occasional power. I remember many times when He helped me through very tough ordeals. But I wasn't hungering and thirsting for righteousness (or a tight, dependent relationship with Him). While I don't claim to have it all together, I can say with confidence I desire, more than anything in my life, to be in a dependent relationship with Him. The challenge is always to remain in "four-wheel-drive" connection.

RELATIONSHIP DEVELOPS FROM DEPENDENCE

The reliance of a child on its mother begins at birth. As the mother nurtures, feeds, and loves her little infant, it learns to be more and more trusting and dependent on the mother's ability to care for it. A love relationship grows and flourishes between mother and child, unlike any other relationship on earth. A growing dependence leads to a growing love relationship.

A newborn's dependence on its mother reminds me of the discussion that Jesus had with Nicodemus, recorded in John 3. "Very truly I tell you, no one can see the kingdom of God unless they are born again" (verse 3). Why didn't Jesus just say you need to be transformed or changed, or even receive a new heart? Why did He say we needed to be "born again"? At birth we are completely reliant on our parents. When we are born again we experience again such dependence—this time on Jesus.

Unlike being born in the flesh, where we move from total dependence to maturity (independence), when we are born of the Spirit we begin a spiritual lifetime of dependence. "Flesh gives birth to flesh, but the Spirit gives birth to spirit" (verse 6). In the flesh we learn to be able to do things on our own such as walking, talking, etc. In the Spirit, however, we are a dependent newborn who grows into a dependent, full-grown servant, never needing to be independent of God's presence or influence.

As the newborn child develops a relationship with its mother, the born-again Christian also embarks on a relationship with Jesus. This love and dependence initially may be limited. Experiencing the blessing and security of trusting Jesus in small things, a Christian sees love grow as well as a desire for more. With continued growth in dependence, love and relationship grow. This naturally occurs in a human child at birth as it sees the mother attend to every physical need. The spiritual rebirth follows the same process.

This was not the original plan. Adam and Eve were able to walk and talk in the Garden of Eden with God. Then came sin, and, except for the few years that Jesus was on earth, we have had a limited ability to interact with God in person.

In order for God to have a true relationship with us He has to start somewhere. Unfortunately we cannot see the tenderness in His eyes, take a walk in the forest with Him, or do many of the things with Him that we do with other people when we are developing a relationship. We cannot see Him cry when we cry or cheer when we cheer. Since we have difficulty grasping the abstract, He begins our relationship with Him on grounds that we can understand—how He lovingly cares for us, better than the best earthly mother would ever think of caring for her newborn.

Jesus wants an intimate relationship with us more than anything else. He created us for relationship; He came to die for us and show the truth about God so we could have this connection with Him, and He is coming back so He can continue a relationship with us for the rest of eternity. Dependence is necessary so that we can learn to love and cherish that relationship with Him. As we begin to depend on Jesus, we see the amazing things He does and start to have a true love for Him. It continues to grow only as we put complete trust in Him.

This kind of dependence does not develop overnight. It can take months and years of discerning His voice, practicing submission through trial and error, learning that each of us really has no strength outside of God's strength, and that the power of Jesus can accomplish literally anything! Jesus likened faith to a mustard seed. It starts as a small kernel of trust; and when one sees how God is faithful, that little bit of trust sprouts and begins to grow (Matt. 13:31, 32). As God continues to show Himself faithful, and a Christian continues to search for God with all their heart, the trust-seedling grows and blossoms into full trust and dependence on God.

CHAPTER 8

HOW DO WE PROTECT OUR RELATIONSHIP WITH JESUS?

If you are married or dating, think back to when your relationship began. The most important part of those first weeks, months, and even years was the relationship forming between the two of you as you grew to care for each other. As the relationship continued, you reached a point of either formally or informally agreeing to do certain things to preserve the special character of your friendship. You agreed not to see others, to spend special times together, and to avoid making other things more important than time spent with each other.

When I married my wife, we agreed that no other person would be more important than each other. We agreed that we would avoid things that would hinder our growth together, including images or pictures of others that could affect our thoughts toward each other. We would protect the name and reputation of the other. We also promised to make special time for each other. Doesn't that sound like the first four commandments? (1) Have no other gods before Me; (2) Have no idols, or things that would hinder growth together; (3) Don't take the name of the Lord in vain; (4) Remember the Sabbath, a special time to spend together (Ex. 20:3-11).

Some think the commandments are just a bunch of restrictions. If I concluded that the agreements between my wife and me were just a bunch of restrictions that she placed on me, you would wonder about my commitment to her, as you should! The key is that I am married and have made a commitment to my wife. We have a covenant relationship. Outside of marriage, those restrictions would be unreasonable and uncalled for. But in the marriage relationship restrictions are necessary to promote a safe environment for our love to grow.

If I am not making her the most important woman in my life, if I'm looking at pornography, talking her down in the presence of others, making no time for her, lying to her, committing adultery, or hurting those she loves, our relationship won't grow and would likely end in divorce. In the same way, the commandments provide a safe environment for our love of God and others to grow, and they protect us from severing our relational commitments to God. The relationship has to come first or the restrictions are just a bunch of rules.

What about the new covenant? We aren't really under the law anymore, are we? While we are not under the law in the sense of being saved by obeying it, we are still asked to obey the law because it is a safety net to protect our dependent relationship with Jesus. When we are fully surrendered to the Spirit's promptings we remain inside the boundaries of the Ten Commandments. When we are living by God's Spirit of love, observing the commandments will be natural. "This is the covenant that I will make with the house of Israel after those days, says the Lord: I will put My laws in their mind, and write them on their hearts; and I will be their God, and they shall be My people" (Heb. 8:10, NKJV). When the laws are in our minds and written on our hearts, we are not "under" the law; it is as much a part of us as breathing.

Let me go back to the marriage relationship. My wife could tell me, "If you love me, you will not make other women more important than me. You will not sacrifice our special times together. You will not look at other women with a romantic interest." These are natural boundaries. These boundaries are not burdensome or restrictive if I love my wife. I am not "under" these laws, because I have a special relationship with her. I would be "under" the law if I was not content in my marriage and was tempted to look around.

"For this is the love of God, that we keep his commandments. And his commandments are not burdensome" (1 John 5:3, RSV). The commandments are no more burdensome for an individual looking to have a dependent relationship with God than are the relational rules that my wife and I have. The key is the committed and preserved relationship. Natural boundaries are necessary to ensure that my heart remains centered on my blossoming relationship with Him.

A married couple I know has had problems because relational rules have not been followed by one of the parties. The husband has not made his wife the most important woman in his life, has not given up pornography, has not told the truth, and has not kept their marriage bed pure. Do you think there have been problems between the two? Of course there have!

What about grace in such a situation? Grace has to do with love, relationship, and forgiveness, not about following rules for the sake of the rules. But there is a need for individuals to make the relationship more important than the things that will/would tear the marriage apart. Marriage is a fully committed, loving relationship between two individuals. There is no way a married couple can have a truly loving and fulfilling relationship without following the equivalent relational rules of the Ten Commandments. If an individual considers the relationship worth preserving he or she will follow the relational rules to protect that relationship; if not, the relationship eventually dies, even in the face of forgiveness (grace) on the part of the injured partner.

When a heart commitment and true love are nurtured between the two parties, there is no need for the laws to be spelled out. When one party has an eye on other women or men and is not acting out the loving part of a spouse, the relational rules are necessary to redirect that person either back to their spouse or fully away from the relationship.

If a marriage is maintained by following relational rules, can we expect less in our friendship with God? Either we are in a fully loving, dependent relationship with Him or we are not. If we are, our full desire is to be like Him, and we joyfully follow the laws He has given. On the other hand, if we are not fully committed to Him the law reminds us that there are things that will hurt our alliance. Looking again at Galatians 3:19, "Why, then, was the law given at all?" we understand it was added to protect our relationship when we are not fully committed or to bring us back when we stray from it. Paul puts it this way: "We know that the law is good if one uses it properly. We also know that law is made not for the righteous but for lawbreakers and rebels" (1 Tim. 1:8).

As in marriage, if we truly love God we will live by the relational rules He has made. "If you love me, keep my commandments" (John 14:15, KJV).

This is not a legalistic following of rules just for the sake of rules; it is a following of the rules for the sake of preserving relationship. Any other reason for obeying the rules is pharasaism. The notion of our being under grace and no longer needing to obey the rules is a terrible fallacy. If we stray from the relationship we need something to remind us when we have wandered, then we can go back and fix the problem. The law has nothing to do with the solution; it is only the mirror reflecting the problem. After realizing there is a problem, we ask for divine help to resolve the relationship issue.

In a number of places Jesus is referred to as the bridegroom and we (the church) are referred to as the bride. When we enter into that marriage agreement with Him, we certainly want to follow certain guidelines to keep the relationship special. My wife doesn't need to remind me to refrain from chasing other women because I love her and do not want to spoil the singular focus of our relationship. Likewise, when we are living by the Spirit and cherish the distinctive friendship we enjoy with Him in our hearts, we are not living "under" the law. We are living under the new covenant, with His laws written in our minds and on our hearts.

I find it interesting that God didn't outline the Ten Commandments immediately after delivering the children of Israel from slavery. He deliberately started with a revelation of His character, developing trust, then dependence, and ultimately a relationship with them. He revealed to them that He was all-powerful, trustworthy, and concerned with their welfare. The Sabbath commandment is the most relational commandment of them all! It calls for a time and space carved from the daily schedule to rest, reflect on God's blessings, and then to relate to Him with thanksgiving.

The preface to the Ten Commandments states: "And God spoke all these words, saying, 'I am the Lord your God, who brought you out of the land of Egypt, out of the house of bondage'" (Ex. 20:1, 2, RSV). In other words, He told them, *I brought you out of slavery and you belong to Me. We have a relationship established, and because of this you need to follow these commands.*

Not only had God shown that He wanted Israel in a relationship with Him, He outlined how they could be fully restored back to Him when they failed. They had celebrated the Passover on their last day in slavery. Each household had sacrificed a perfect lamb, and the blood placed on their doorposts. This symbolism pointed forward to Jesus, the perfect Lamb, dying on the cross, slain for our deliverance from sin.

When we accept that perfect gift, willingly placing the blood on our heart's door, we are delivered from our slavery—living apart from God in sin. After our deliverance we begin the journey to our Promised Land. Like the children of Israel, Christians encounter many trials along the way, and it may seem God isn't with us. We often murmur about the rough times, but in retrospect, we may see God's leading and His mercy shining through the darkness.

"During all the wanderings of Israel, Christ, in the pillar of cloud and of fire, was their Leader. While there were types pointing to a Savior to come, there was also a present Savior, who gave commands to Moses for the people, and who was set forth before them as the only channel of blessing" (*Patriarchs and Prophets*, p. 311).

While the Israelites looked forward to the Savior, they were to be aware of God's continual presence and saving power.

God moved the children of Israel to Sinai and gave them the Ten Commandments as a protection for the relationship He wanted with them. First, He protected the dependent relationship between Himself and them; then He provided protection of their relationships with each other. Jesus summed up the first four commandments, as did Moses: "Love the Lord your God with all your heart and with all your soul and with all your strength and with all your mind." Then, regarding the last six: "Love your neighbor as yourself" (Luke 10:27; Deut. 6:5).

God knew preserving the relationship with Him was most important, so He gave the first four instructions outlining how to accomplish that. He also knew we wouldn't have a lasting, dependent relationship with Him if we were not treating His other children with the same love He has for them, so He defined the last six commandments.

Today, by God's grace, we are saved from our past transgressions through the cross. But His saving power does not stop there. His presence and power continually help us overcome the devil in the present. "He will save his people from their sins" (Matt. 1:21, RSV). This does not say "from their past sins"; it says "from their sins," implying present and future sins. Though not a visible presence, as He was to the children of Israel, He is there just the same. He is still "Immanuel," which means "God with us" (Matt. 1:23). He continues to be our leader and Savior in the moment-to-moment struggles with Satan, who is working through our flesh.

Dependence also defines the concept of right and wrong. Something is right if it is done as God asked and is done in the right heart, not just the right action. If the right action is done in independence, or something from my own strength, that is sin. If the right thing is done outside of my own strength, in His, it is righteousness.

Again, God did not begin with giving the Ten Commandments at Sinai. He initiated a relationship with Israel in Egypt, demonstrating His love and devotion. He established His sovereignty by orchestrating events that were completely inconceivable in human terms. God provided evidence that all the gods of the Egyptians were impotent against His power. He exhibited that He was trustworthy, keeping His promises to Abraham, Isaac, and Jacob. He provided reconciliation and redemption through the Passover. Then He asked for their dependence on Him to leave Egypt. As they moved through the desert, He continued to show His providence and provision, always guiding and leading them.

CHAPTER 9

CAN WE MAKE DEPENDENCE EASIER?

After receiving the Ten Commandments on tablets of stone, Moses climbed back up Mount Sinai, into the cloud with God, where he received specific instructions on how to build the tabernacle. God wanted a spot where His presence could be seen and felt by the Israelites as well as those who came to visit their camp. Detailed blueprints were given so the earthly temple would be a replica of the one in heaven (Heb. 8:5).

After the tabernacle was reverently built according to His explicit plan, God's holy presence filled the tent-building (Ex. 40:34, 35). Every article of furniture in the tabernacle pointed to Christ and His sacrifice, reminding the priests and everyone in the camp of the importance of their coming Redeemer. Also, in the tabernacle the will of God was often communicated to the people through the high priest or a prophet.

"There I will meet with you and speak to you; there also I will meet with the Israelites, and the place will be consecrated by my glory. . . . They will know that I am the Lord their God, who brought them out of Egypt so that I might dwell among them. I am the Lord their God" (Ex. 29:42-45).

Again God reminded the Israelites that He was their deliverer and therefore had begun a relationship with them. For this reason He was establishing a place where He could dwell with them and communicate with them.

Years later God instructed Solomon on the building of a stationary Temple. When the Babylonians destroyed it, another was built. Each Temple was a reminder of God's presence and His grace in reaching out to humanity with forgiveness. When Christ died, the Temple's purpose of pointing forward to His sacrifice was fulfilled, and with the spreading of the gospel to the Gentiles, there was no longer a need for a centralized spot where God would dwell among mankind. Instead, with the coming of the Holy Spirit, God gave humans the awesome privilege of being His temple (1 Cor. 6:19, 20).

Should the purpose of our temples be any different than that of the original Temple?

- A spot where God's presence can be seen and felt.
- Every article in it a reminder of Christ's sacrifice for us.
- The site where God's will is revealed to His people.

Through our lives, God's presence should be seen and felt. Our thoughts and actions should remind us—and others—of Christ's presence and sacrifice for us. We should be the place where God's will is revealed.

My wife has coached young teenagers in a skit dealing with our willingness to allow Jesus to make the decisions in our life. The teen playing the part of Christ was asked if his role felt like a big responsibility. His response was an emphatic "Yes!" As temples, we should have that same sense of gravity in portraying God and pointing to Christ.

"What was it that drew men to Jesus? . . . The one thing that men could not ignore was the compassion and love that came from his heart and on to his face and into his words and deeds. If we abide in him as he abides in us, we begin to see things differently. We begin to look at things with his eyes" (Bob Benson, *NIV Men's Devotional Bible*, p. 1064).

Running on a hotel treadmill one day, I tried to look somewhere besides at my reflection in the bank of mirrors in front of me. However, each time I looked away, my feet would stray to one side or the other. Finally I glanced up and asked God to show me a picture of Jesus. It then came to me: If I am a temple, reflecting Jesus as everything in the Temple did, looking in my own eyes should portray the face and temperament of Jesus. Responsibility? Wow!

SUBDIVISIONS OF LIFE

Many times we compartmentalize our lives: work, play, secular, spiritual, etc. As we are temples of the Holy Spirit, God desires for us to realize that every activity we engage in is a spiritual experience. That would include driving, taking out the trash, exercising, reading. Everything will be done through our connection with Him and for His glory. When we embrace this concept and determine to live in His presence every moment, we enter an intimacy with Him that is holy—truly being a temple.

LOVE IN ACTION

In order for us to be the site where God's presence is seen and felt, we must be different from the world. The selfish ambitions of the world are replaced by an others-centered focus (Phil. 2:3, 4.) This involves accepting an attitude of dependence, of crucifying the spirit of independence and self-centeredness. John repeatedly tells us in his writings how we are to stand out from those of the world—through love.

"Love comes from God. Everyone who loves has been born of God and knows God. Whoever does not love does not know God, because God is love" (1 John 4:7, 8). "Dear children, let us not love with words or speech but with actions and in truth" (1 John 3:18).

In everyday language that means I am to love and serve even those who do not help me meet my goals (even if I perceive them to be God's goals). I am to love those who hurt and demean me—or others. I am to love the boss who unfairly calls me into the office to discuss a situation for which I was not responsible. Anyone who comes into my circle of acquaintances or dealings needs my unconditional love. If we are God's temple, the site where others can see and feel God's presence, we have to be loving in "actions and in truth."

Dependence is the avenue to a loving attitude and response to others, even in the face of adversity. As we fully depend on God, our natural response of protecting ourselves at all costs is subdued and even lost. We are freed to see others as God sees them instead of as a threat to our convenience or efficiency. We are able to perceive, through the Spirit, what individuals may need from us, making us loving toward all.

Jesus calls us to be the light of the world. Light and darkness—polar opposites. Light obliterates darkness, but darkness can do nothing to light. We are to be 100 percent different from the world, not 50 percent or even 98 percent. When our light shines, it obliterates the darkness of conflict, independence, self-centeredness, etc. The light of His love will be noticeable anywhere and anytime.

Where do loving feelings and attitudes come from? Hard work? No. "Can an Ethiopian change his skin or a leopard its spots? Neither can you do good who are accustomed to doing evil" (Jer. 13:23). In other words we cannot do this on our own. We need the change of heart David prayed for in Psalm 51:10-12: "Create in me a pure heart, O God, and renew a steadfast spirit within me. . . . Grant me a willing spirit, to sustain me." The only way to have this change in heart is through a willing spirit in which God can place His love. Only then can we love others unconditionally as He has loved us.

HUMILITY

Though we have already talked about humility, I want to briefly revisit it in the context of what would make us different as a temple of God. God reveals the attitude He wants through His temples.

"These are the ones I look on with favor: those who are humble and contrite in spirit" (Isa. 66:2). "I live . . . also with the one who is contrite and lowly in spirit, to revive the spirit of the lowly and to revive the heart of the contrite" (Isa. 57:15).

Pride, a haughty attitude, and arrogance are part of independence, or living outside a dependent relationship with God. As the dependent relationship with God must precede all other parts of our relationship with Him, pride, haughtiness, and arrogance all prevent that from happening. Thus they lie at the root of our relational problems with God and ultimately with others as well.

DEPENDENCE LEADS TO CHANGE

If we are searching for God with all our heart, then listening to and hearing God's voice, will there be changes in our life? There is no doubt we will be encouraged and convicted to make adjustments so that our outward appearance becomes more like that of a true temple, reflecting Jesus in all aspects of living. Where those changes are initiated and where the power comes from is key! They come from an ever-deepening, dependent relationship with Jesus. As we progress from an understanding of God's sovereignty and goodness toward us to a committed, depending, listening, following relationship with Jesus, there is no way we will not be changed into His likeness.

Unfortunately, many want to jump over the arduous and sometimes painstaking steps of finding the close walking and talking relationship with Jesus and go straight to the visible changes. These attempts to make visible changes without the relationship with Jesus are self-generated attempts. God has a progression of steps He leads us through, and the first place that the path leads is to Himself, not to externals.

The Israelites were told not to defile the Temple, sometimes at the cost of death. Is the same true for us? "Don't you know that you yourselves are God's temple and that God's Spirit dwells in your midst? If anyone destroys God's temple, God will destroy that person; for God's temple is sacred, and you together are that temple" (1 Cor. 3:16, 17). If we are not caring for our temple physically or spiritually, can we expect any other outcome than ultimate destruction? It all comes back to the first thing that God tried to accomplish with the children of Israel—fostering a dependent relationship. If we are trying in our own strength to be loving or to clear our minds of worldly influences, are we truly fulfilling the purpose of the temple? If we attempt to keep the temple from defilement without a God-relationship giving us the power to stay pure and undefiled, then we are doing it for the sake of the law and not for the sake of God and His purposes. Those who do anything without God's power will find themselves in sync with the five foolish virgins, who had no oil at the time of the Bridegroom's appearing. Without the Holy Spirit in our lives prompting us along the path of righteousness, we will hear, with the five foolish virgins, "I don't know you" (Matt. 25:12), i.e., "*You never had a relationship with Me.*"

HEALTHY RELATIONSHIPS NECESSITATE HEALTHY BODIES

After God delivered the Israelites from slavery, He gave them the Ten Commandments for relationship preservation, provided instructions on constructing the tabernacle, and gave them stipulations on health. Maintaining wellness makes it possible to function as the temple of the Holy Spirit. As temples, our bodies and minds should be optimally maintained so we can hear the slightest whisperings of the Spirit to our conscience.

God knew it was going to be important for the Hebrews to be in good physical health in order to finish their trip to the Promised Land and conquer the giants in the land (though obviously that would be through His power). They were to be full of vigor and lacking disease so that the surrounding countries would observe and want to emulate them. The Lord promised: "If you will diligently hearken to the voice of the Lord your God, and do that which is right in his eyes, and give heed to his commandments and keep all his statutes, I will put none of the diseases upon you which I put upon the Egyptians; for I am the Lord, your healer" (Ex. 15:26, RSV).

You see, God wanted the children of Israel to have the best of relations with Him and with others. He wanted them to feel good and be vigorous into old age. Jesus said it this way: "I came that they may have life, and have it abundantly" (John 10:10, RSV). In other words, "*I want you to have a good life and then live it to its fullest.*"

When I became fully aware of these concepts through the prompting of the Holy Spirit, I realized I was not the picture of health I should have been. At the time I was carrying extra weight and did not exercise regularly. My water intake and diet weren't optimal. Though I understood health principles, I thought that avoiding tobacco, alcohol, illicit drugs, and caffeine was all I needed to do to maintain adequate health as God's temple. After all, I was functioning well—unless I was taxed physically, and I blamed that on my increasing years!

When God brings to our consciousness things in our lives not in submission to Him, we have the option to follow His leading (our faith in response to His promptings) or continue living in the flesh. God led me to start exercising regularly, improve my diet, drink more water, and drop some weight. Do you think I felt better physically as well as feeling more positive about myself? You bet I did—and I still do! Do you think it was easy to start exercising when I hadn't had an exercise program for at least 20 years? Was it easy to gradually change my diet? No, not at the time—and occasionally it still isn't easy to continue. But in the end, has God's promise of having a better life been fulfilled? Yes!

When God prompts us to change, the devil makes the changes seem impossible (and they often are in our own power), and then we shrink from the task because of the self-sacrifice required. If we persevere through His strength, we emerge from the struggle better off and still in communion with Him. If we decide that the struggle is too much, if we are not responding to His presence and promptings with faith, eventually we may either drift from our relationship with Him or, by His grace, listen the next time He convicts us. If we repeatedly choose not to respond to God's continual presence (His grace) and promptings in faith (our positive response to Him) and if we persist in our rebellion (actions against His will), it will eventually separate us from Him.

So how are we to live and what are we to look like as healthy specimens acting as God's temple? To be able to live as the temple of the Holy Spirit, we need to be in optimal condition physically, mentally, and spiritually. If any one of the three is lacking, we will be unable to function optimally as a temple. We will not have clear minds to hear God speaking with us, and we will not be an example to lead others to a relationship with Jesus. Areas we need to honestly evaluate through the Holy Spirit's guidance include food, alcohol, tobacco, caffeine, exercise, obesity, endurance, clear thinking, clear conscience, and a peaceful demeanor.

If we are fully honest, we Christians often look no different from those around us in many ways, including weight, modesty, arrogance, etc. God has given us a road map of how we can be the happiest, how we can commune with Him best, and how we can be the best influence on others. It's not an easy path to change, but again we are not doing the work of changing—we are listening to the influence of the Holy Spirit. When we meet temptations, we can claim the promise of James 4:7, 8: "Submit yourselves, then, to God. Resist the devil, and he will flee from you. Come near to God and he will come near to you."

Our journey with God goes from relationship to protection of relationship. Then we look and act more like the temple we are becoming through changes happening inwardly, which eventually show up on the outside. Outward change is not to make others believe we have achieved inward change. God doesn't desire outward change only; He's looking for those who are "circumcised" in heart, in relation to the covenant with Him (Deut. 30:6). God does not want us to have "a form of godliness but denying its power" (2 Tim. 3:5). He desires godliness because we have His power to overcome the devil. The road still starts at dependence and relationship first.

CHAPTER 10

DO YOU KNOW YOUR ABCS?

When a trauma victim comes into the emergency room, the staff follows an orderly protocol to evaluate the patient so that the most important things for survival are not missed because of distracting injuries. These are called the ABCs of trauma care. "A" stands for airway, "B" for breathing, "C" for circulation, and so on. At each level, care for a particular issue needs to be completed before going on to the next step in the evaluation. Whenever something in the patient's status worsens, we must go back to the beginning (or "A," the airway) and then progress through the protocol, completing the care for each problem before progressing to the next item. This ensures that something didn't change that could produce a life-threatening complication.

In the same way we must start with the ABCs of Christianity when we are dealing with a victim traumatized by the devil's attacks (whether it is ourselves or someone else). "A" is for the accepting relationship we have with Jesus. We accept that we are unable to do anything except submit to Him through our will. We accept that He is sovereign and wants to communicate His will to us through multiple avenues. We accept that it is not about us, but about Him.

"B" is for the boundaries that we set up to protect that growing relationship with Jesus. "C" is for communicating our status with Jesus to others through our appearance and demeanor. Everything in our life takes on the light that dispels darkness. The temple of the Holy Spirit here is doing the same job as the original—everything in it points to Jesus.

"D" is the protection of the temple of God through diet and exercise, facilitating the desired continuous communion with God. By optimizing diet, exercise, and other basic health principles we avoid the poor health of mind or body that can break down lines of communication.

When "A," the accepting relationship (or dependence), is growing, one can go on to "B," the protection of that all-important accepting relationship. When the accepting relationship is protected through God's power, it is then possible to progress to "C," taking on the communication responsibilities of the temple and being the light that dispels darkness. "D" follows with the protection of the temple through the health laws, thus making the continuous communion with God uninhibited by poor health of mind or body.

As with a trauma victim, if at any time an individual's experience deteriorates, the goal is not to correct that person's lifestyle with health changes, the symbolism found in the sanctuary service, or the Ten Commandments. Rather, people must go back to the first step of recommitting everything they are and have to Him, then bow in dependence to His will and purpose for their lives, going back to that accepting relationship. Things can then again progress back down the ABCs, but they always start with "A," returning to "A" if there are problems.

When we consider what is most important to study and dwell on it in Bible study and prayer, it would seem obvious that we would start with "A" and then move to "B," and so on. It would follow that when we encourage others or evangelize, we would also start with "A," as "B," "C," and "D" make no difference without establishing "A" first. The step of most importance should be addressed most often and with the most vigor.

KEEP THE MAIN THING THE MAIN THING

In a hospital setting it is always easy to let one's attention be diverted to nonlife-threatening problems. A fracture that has punctured through the skin or an amputated little finger are important injuries that need to be cared for, but they cannot take attention away from the life-threatening problems of a closed airway, lack of breathing, or circulatory collapse. Action must be directed to the life-threatening problems first, which is the reason for the ABCs of trauma care.

We are all in a life-threatening situation with regard to sin. Unless we remain focused on what is most important in our spiritual life, we might lose that life forever. We should not concentrate on the minor aspects of Christianity because there is so much to be done to resolve our independent separation from God. Though an amputated little finger is not a trivial thing, when it is compared with the complete loss of life it assumes a relatively minor position. Our time in Bible study and prayer needs to be centered on God, where our problems with sin and separation can be cared for. Our problems with separation from God cannot be addressed by health reform, controversies about prophecy, end-time events, Bible trivia, or even the symbolism of the sanctuary service. Our separation issues can be rectified only by humbly submitting to God and learning dependence on Him.

I have been approached on more than one occasion by well-meaning individuals about different religious topics outside of the ABCs mentioned above. They were matters that did not apply to my daily Christian walk and were more theoretical than fully grounded in Scripture. My response was that I had too much work learning God's will for me in the ABCs of salvation to deal with matters that were not central to the themes He has set as priorities for me to learn about. As Paul says, do not "devote [ourselves] to myths and endless genealogies. Such things promote controversial speculations rather than advancing God's work—which is by faith" (1 Tim. 1:4).

CONSERVATIVES VERSUS LIBERALS

When people stray off the center of the road to the right, or the conservative side, things such as the law, sanctuary service, or health laws seem to dictate their lives. They get stuck in a rut of externals, where "doing" things or "understanding" certain concepts becomes the most important part of their experience. The commandments must be kept to the letter. The symbolism of the sanctuary service must be fully understood because it is the true way to salvation. Health laws must be kept or one will never be able to enter the kingdom.

Then there's the left, or liberal, side of the road. Here relationship without responsibility is often seen. God's grace covers all, so all we need to do is accept that grace to be saved.

Is there truth on either side of the road? Of course there is! The commandments, sanctuary service, and health laws are all important. There is also a great need for God's abundant grace and mercy. But each is just a small piece of gold—in the center of the road is rock-solid gold from which the little nuggets found on the sides of the road originated. This center-of-the-road, pure stuff is the life-changing truth of a dependence on God that transforms us. It changes us from being mere dust to being a light to the world. It is having the "power," not just a "form of godliness" (2 Tim. 3:5).

If our church is dying, it is because we are walking on the sides of the road; we have no true gold purified by our dependence on Him. When we stay focused on the heart of God, we encounter the cross, which is seen in its full splendor only in the center of the road. It is there we develop the perfect, dependent, personal relationship with our Creator, Savior, and King. Jesus hung at the center of the three crosses; either we are in the center or we are not on track with Him and His plans for us.

The devil does not care which side of the road you may wander; he just wants you distracted from the central character of Jesus. Once we are growing in the dependent relationship with Him, then we can use the help provided to maintain that precious relationship—the protective commandments, the temple where we allow His love to shine through us, and good health to continually hear His voice and carry out His purposes. If we don't know His voice, what good will it do us to hear it? If we don't understand what God wants to do in our personal life to make us like Him, the sanctuary service is useless. If I do not have the relationship, I have no need to protect it with the commandments. If I am depending on mercy alone and God's forbearance of my sinful nature, I am not depending on His power or allowing Him to change me to be like Him.

CHAPTER 11

DO YOU CELEBRATE DEPENDENCE DAY?

INDEPENDENCE DAY VERSUS DEPENDENCE DAY

In the United States, as in many countries, we celebrate Independence Day—a time commemorating our nation's freedom. Unfortunately, we celebrate not only our nation's independence but our own. What we really need to observe is "dependence day"!

We usually do not label Easter with that term, but at its root it is a time of commemorating dependence. Not the bunnies-and-candy sort of celebration, but rather recalling the Creator-God who chose dependence on His Father in the Garden of Gethsemane rather than His own way. It is clear that Jesus did not want to experience separation from the Father. He asked three times if there was another way to accomplish the goal. He was in such anguish over the widening chasm between Him and His Father as He took on my sins and yours, that He sweat great drops of blood. This was *not* what He wanted, but He submitted His own will to the Father's: "My Father, if it is not possible for this cup to be taken away unless I drink it, may your will be done" (Matt. 26:42).

Notice, not may *My* will be done, but *Your* will be done. Even during the ensuing torture and ridicule, He accepted all that happened in full dependence on His Father; the mission that had been drafted long before could not be aborted. Good Friday became a day of true dependence, and the resulting power of that decision of dependence was demonstrated on Resurrection Sunday.

Paul understood this dependence holiday. "That I may know him and the power of his resurrection, and may share his sufferings, becoming like him in his death, that if possible I may attain the resurrection from the dead" (Phil. 3:10, 11, RSV).

Paul wanted to *know* Jesus, to *know* the power of His resurrection, and to share in His sufferings, becoming dependent on Him like He was in His death. This desire of Paul came through the pure and undefiled dependent

70

faith that Jesus had. The power from that dependence will result in Paul's resurrection from the dead.

KNOWN IN HELL

Paul was so filled with the Holy Spirit that hell trembled.
Paul was centered in the Spirit—
there were no side issues.
He spent no time defending the edges of his life.
It really didn't matter.
One thing mattered, that was all . . .

He had no ambitions for himself—only Christ's cause,
so he had nothing to be jealous of.
He had no reputation,
so he didn't have to fight for himself.
He had no possessions,
so there were no things to worry about.
He had no rights,
so he could suffer no wrongs.
He was already broken,
so no one could break him.
He had already died,
so no one could kill him.
He was less than the least,
so who could embarrass him?
He had suffered the loss of all things,
so who could rob him?
He was totally Christ's,
so no one could take him.

It's no wonder Heaven loved him
and hell feared him.
When we live like Paul
hell will tremble,
and we will not be focused on ourselves,
but on God.

—J. Wallace Hamilton
adapted by Ron Halversen, Jr.
used by permission of Ron Halversen, Jr.

What more could be said about Paul's dependence on God? He took nothing for himself; he gave everything to his loving, eternal Comforter, Friend, Creator, and Savior through his dependent faith!

DEPENDENCE AWAKENING

Rappelling off Corona Arch near Moab, Utah, gave me a radically different viewpoint of dependence than I had ever experienced. It was my turn to rappel down the 120-foot arch where only the top 20 feet offered a sidewall on which to position my feet. On the remaining 100 feet I would have only a rope to support my descent. Though the arch was high, it seemed extremely high, for it is situated hundreds of feet above the valley floor. This, combined with a rappel that was almost twice my highest previous distance, made me more than a little nervous.

Also, several of those who went before me were very wary, and their fear added to my anxiety. When it was my turn, my knees began to shake. I clipped in to the edge protection rope before attaching my rappelling ropes. Though I was still a little nervous, getting attached to the ropes and starting the descent eased my fear somewhat. But it wasn't until I was hanging by the rope and not supporting myself on the sidewall that I felt completely comfortable and without fear.

When I was completely in control of the circumstances in a relatively dangerous situation (at the top of the arch) and not attached to the rappelling rope, I was the most fearful. After attaching to my rappelling rope but still slightly in control by pushing off the sidewall with my feet, I was still nervous in my descent. Not until all of my weight was on the rope and I was not being assisted at all was I completely without fear. Only then was I truly depending on the rope for my complete safety.

The spiritual parallels of this experience sent me to my knees. In life, when I am not hooked into my rappelling rope support (Jesus), I have no peace and the worries of life seem insurmountable. When my rappelling rope is clipped in and supporting me but I'm still doing some of the work, I am not completely at peace. It is only when I am fully supported by Jesus and His care for me and not trying to make things happen at all that I am fully at peace. Conversely, when I am not fully at peace or have anxiety about anything, I know that I am not maintaining a dependent attitude on Jesus.

This could be a useful method for checking your personal dependence quotient. In order for us to have an inner peace when fully supported by

Jesus, we must know from the depths of our soul that not only can He support us, but that He will and desires to be always at our side. Ken Sande, in *Peacemakers*, reminds us that "God is both sovereign and good" (p. 65). He can work all things out for our good, and according to Romans 8:28, He wants to. Why should we then want to rappel alone, controlling things on our own?

CHAPTER 12

WHAT HAPPENS
WHEN WE DEPEND ON JESUS?

WHAT DEPENDENCE DOES FOR US

"Do not be anxious about anything, but in every situation, by prayer and petition, with thanksgiving, present your requests to God. And the peace of God, which transcends all understanding, will guard your hearts and your minds in Christ Jesus" (Phil. 4:6, 7).

When we are fully dependent on Jesus, understanding that "in all things God works for the good of those who love him, who have been called according to His purpose" (Rom. 8:28), we are at peace—a peace that transcends all understanding.

Paul tells us not to be anxious about *anything*. That means no anxiety about health problems, work issues, money matters, family concerns—not anxious about anything. Then David says in Psalm 112:7, 8: "They will have no fear of bad news; their hearts are steadfast, trusting in the Lord. Their hearts are secure, they will have no fear." To have that sort of peace we must be totally dependent on His power moment by moment. This kind of peace is one of the benefits of dependence that people everywhere would like to experience.

Peace must be an important thing to God. Most of the recorded encounters with heavenly beings in the Bible include "Peace be with you." Each time Jesus visited with the disciples after His crucifixion He used the same phrase: "Peace be with you." Peace is frequently referenced in Isaiah and the Gospels. Almost every letter in the New Testament has a greeting and/or ending that includes "peace." Paul even calls God the "God of peace" (1 Thess. 5:23). Jesus said in John 16:33, "I have told you these things, so that in me you may have peace."

Why is peace so important to God? When I am at peace I am not worried about the past, the present, or the future. I am content, fully trusting and depending on my sovereign Savior. Even when life is worrisome He is beside me, providing for and protecting me. With this promise I can give up my self-centered rush for things or prestige. I am peacefully and humbly resting in His will and allowing His purposes to be worked out for my benefit. I am depending on Him completely.

We worry when we forget about His past leadings and pull our hand out of His, trying to manage problems on our own. The Hebrews did this, and they had no peace or rest. In the desert they were constantly murmuring about things they might lack in the near future, but these fears did not materialize.

"I have taken away my peace from this people. . . . 'Why has the Lord pronounced all this great evil against us?' . . . 'Because your fathers have forsaken me, says the Lord, and have gone after other gods and have served and worshipped them, and have forsaken me and have not kept my law, and because you have done worse than your fathers, for behold, every one of you follows his stubborn evil will, refusing to listen to me'" (Jer.16:5-12, RSV).

"But the wicked are like the tossing sea, which cannot rest, whose waves cast up mire and mud. 'There is no peace,' says my God, 'for the wicked'" (Isa. 57:20, 21). The "wicked" mentioned here are the opposite of the righteous—those who have a close, daily, dependent relationship with God. The wicked, then, are those who do not have a loving, dependent relationship with God. They do not have true peace because they do not have the assurance that God is there, moment by moment, guiding them and abiding with them.

Without God's peace we worry. We worry about finances, the economy, bank failures, corporate bankruptcy, unemployment, war, AIDS, other viral epidemics, terrorism, new countries with nuclear capabilities, corruption in government, corruption in business, families falling apart, teenage pregnancy, drug abuse in grade and high school, violence in schools and public places, and the list goes on. Does it sound like we have peace, rest, quietness, and trust?

The present generation is the most depressed of any in history. Antidepressant use is unsurpassed and the use of sedatives to ease one's worries is also rampant. Christians are as affected with depression as non-Christians. What is happening? Do we not understand that we have a God who can and will still the storm in us? Perhaps we believe that He can still the storm or quiet us, but we do not act on it or apply it to our lives.

When I was a new medical school graduate in residency, I found myself clinically depressed. I was sleep-deprived, working long hours, and usually rewarded with only criticism. I felt out of control and at the mercy of seemingly unmerciful superiors. I could not see through the present or grasp that this situation was allowed by God to make me a better person in some way. This was one of the most difficult times of my life. I wish I had known then what I now know about dependence.

After two years of seeming helplessness, I regained control of my circumstances and emerged from the depression, though sadly not from my realization of my need for dependence on God. Isaiah 8:22: "They will look toward the earth and see only distress and darkness and fearful gloom, and they will be thrust into utter darkness." Why the darkness and depression? They do not consult their God (verse 19). They fear and are in dread of other things rather than in the Almighty (verses 12, 13).

Satan has counterfeits for every good thing God wants to give us, and the issue of dependence is no different. Independence looks macho and cool. Or, as Frank Sinatra said, "I did it my way." This attitude of independence sounds good when things are going well, but what happens when you lose your job, your child develops brain cancer, your spouse leaves you, the stock market plummets and you have little left, you are a victim of a disaster or crime? When we encounter these trying and worrisome situations without hope of help, it is frightening. It may drive some to the point of suicide. Others use alcohol, drugs, sex, pornography, gambling, and other addictions to take their mind off the present uncertainty or fear.

On the other hand, dependence on God gives us confidence that He knows what He's doing. We don't worry about the future, for He has promised to work all things for our good. There is a quiet, peaceful atmosphere that surrounds such a God-dependent person—a feeling not unlike that of a slave set free!

Do circumstances change because of the dependence? Sometimes. Is there a change in the attitude and a sense of peace because of the dependence? Always!

Peter reminds us to cast all our cares upon Him, for He cares for us (1 Peter 5:7). Jesus tells us, "Peace I leave with you; my peace I give you. I do not give to you as the world gives. Do not let your hearts be troubled and do not be afraid" (John 14:27).

The peace of Christ comes from complete, childlike trust in our sovereign and loving God. This peace does not come from a lack of trials or problems; it results from a pure and complete trust that no matter what happens He will see me through it. Peter tells us to be zealous about being found by Him at peace. Why did Peter want us to be diligent in our pursuit of peace? Peace is a thermometer of our dependence; if we are at peace, God's act of quieting us through dependence is working.

HEALING THROUGH DEPENDENCE

There are three ways that dependence leads to healing. First, as we find our total identity in Christ and repent of our sins, we are no longer separated from Him. The chasm of separation that we experienced from Him is gone, and we are healed spiritually. This is the experience of the paralytic who was let down through the roof by his friends. He wanted physical healing, but he yearned even more for spiritual healing.

Have you ever felt like Jacob, wanting to go back and do things over the right way? Do you want to be forgiven by God and others, then be able to forgive yourself? Depending on Jesus makes this a reality. Of course, there is the "accuser of the brethren" who wants to take this healing away, but we can lean on Jesus and have the full healing that He promises. "Submit yourselves therefore to God. Resist the devil and he will flee from you. Draw near to God and he will draw near to you" (James 4:7, 8, RSV).

Second, dependence leads to healing in our relationships with others. When we fully depend on Jesus we are no longer caught up in the "American dream" of financial success or climbing the economic ladder. As a result, we can give our full love and attention to our family and others around us. When we're not worried about our financial success, we cease being competitors with those around us for "top-dog" status. Instead we see others as costrugglers on the way to the kingdom. When we are not selfishly vying for our own position of power, relationships can be restored and healed through the guidance of the Holy Spirit (whom we are listening to on a continual basis). We no longer have to hold back our apologies for wrongs that we have committed, because we no longer have to protect our ego and self-worth; God is doing that for us!

The third way dependence leads to healing is by true physical healing for one's self or for others. Obviously this isn't something that happens every time we ask, as I noted in the story from Haiti. But miracles of healing still do occur. I will mention three instances in which I have seen physical healing miracles.

There was a man about 50 years old whom I had treated for an ankle fracture with an external fixator (pins placed into bone, which stick out through the skin so that clamps and bars can be added to hold the bones in a certain position). His fracture had healed and the external fixator had been removed. Unfortunately, he kept having infections from one of the sites where a pin had been. When X-rays and blood tests indicated a likely infection at one of the old pin sites, I took him to the operating room to resolve the infection.

In the operating room the orthopedic resident physician (physician in training) and I were cleaning his bone when suddenly his heart quit working properly. There were still attempts at pumping blood, but little blood was being pumped. I immediately started chest compressions to maintain blood flow to his brain and other vital organs while the anesthesiologist gave medications and worked to bring him back. Of course, I started praying right away.

As with almost all patients whom I take care of for any length of time, this man had become a very good friend. We went through three rounds of medications and 10 minutes of chest compressions without success. I was still praying for a miracle. About 12 minutes after arrest, his heart started pumping and maintaining his blood pressure. We finished the surgery quickly and got him out of the operating room, quite sure that he would have severe brain damage because of the amount of time he had compromised blood flow to his brain.

Later that day, when he was fully awake, I discovered he had only a little loss of short-term memory. Wow, what a miracle! First, his heart began functioning after a significant amount of downtime and then he had very minimal neurologic problems. All I could say was that he truly was a "miracle man."

The next experience happened in Fiji. My family and I had gone to help with medical care. I was operating with a Fijian orthopedic surgeon on a man who, while driving his motorcycle, had been hit by a car. He had a thighbone fracture and hip fracture on the same leg. Fortunately (blessing, not coincidence), I had brought along a rod that could be inserted through the knee into the thighbone, as well as a plate with a blade on it that could fix hip fractures.

We placed the femoral rod first and then started on the hip fracture. When we saw the fluoroscopy (immediate X-ray) images in the operating room, it was obvious that there were two fractures in the hip at different levels—a difficult surgery to be done even in the United States under the best of circumstances. I asked for divine help as we started. In order for the hip to be lined up for optimal function and healing after surgery, this "blade plate" needed to be placed precisely at the right spot. The Fijian physician had not placed many of these implants, so I tried to help him put it in. After some time I took over and tried for a long time to place it in the perfect spot, but I just couldn't get it where it belonged. I tried every trick I knew, but it just wouldn't go where it was supposed to sit. Finally we had to accept a suboptimal position for the tip of the blade, making it less likely that the fracture would fully heal.

That night I couldn't sleep. *God, why didn't You help me? With the position of the plate, this fracture isn't going to heal. Then what? The corrective surgery needed is not in the expertise of the locals.* I questioned and agonized about the surgery almost all night.

The next day was my last at this hospital, so I checked on patients and took some final pictures of the work we had done. I went to this young man's bedside and looked at the X-rays that had been taken of the thigh and the hip. To my surprise and amazement, the plate was in the exact spot we had struggled so long to place it. It was perfect!

I was asked if it was possible that the orientation of our X-rays in the operating room made things appear different. I truly did not think that was possible; the difference in position was markedly different and we had moved the fluoroscopy machine into varying angles during the surgery to be sure we were being as accurate as possible. I was s-o-o-o-o thankful! God had come through as my refuge, strength, and fortress.

I hesitate to record this next incident, as it was one of those times when I felt I was truly on holy ground. I've had many people say they were healed by this potion or that, sometimes even calling it miraculous when circumstances actually didn't fit together as a true miracle.

I was reading Mark 2 one Friday evening. For some reason I was actually in the story—I was the paralytic who was being lowered to see Jesus. In my mind I was truly there. Jesus looked at me and told me, "Your sins are forgiven." I could feel relief and peace that was unexplainable. He then looked at me and said something like "You are healed."

For several years I had been dealing with my own intermittent fast heart rate. It usually came on during times of stress. I knew Jesus was referring to this heart problem that I had. As I continued reading I became Matthew at the tax collectors' booth. Jesus came close and said, "Follow Me." At that point I was no longer part of the story but had stepped back into the shoes of the reader.

I knew at this point my heart problem was resolved, that my sins were forgiven, and that I was to follow Jesus. Yes, my heart problem did resolve. Some might argue that it was because of decreased stress, or that it went away on its own, just as it had started spontaneously. Either way, I was healed and remain healed. As I have said before, God doesn't choose to heal everyone; sometimes His answer to our request is "No." When that is the answer it is even more important that we depend on Him fully, though it is harder. "Lord, I believe; help thou my unbelief."

God wants to heal your relationship with Him and with others, and sometimes even you or someone close to you.

FREEDOM IN DEPENDENCE

When are we truly delivered from the slavery of sin? When we are dependent on God for that deliverance. Otherwise we remain in the chains of independence from God—which is really the definition of sin, isn't it? Sin is separation from God, and the independent spirit is nothing less than living in continual separation from Him.

Jesus says in John 8:32 that "you will know the truth, and the truth will make you free" (RSV). The greatest truth is that we have a loving Savior who is sovereign and working out all things for our good. He is not only willing, but wants to bear all of our burdens (Matt. 11:28) and wishes to direct our lives if we will only listen to His guiding. He wants us to be in perfect peace because our hearts are kept in Him and are depending on Him.

We have no worries today because He is guiding. We have no worries about yesterday because our failures have been forgiven. We have no worries about tomorrow because He will lead us in the best path to follow. How much more can He offer? We are faced with the decision to accept His marching orders or reject them, as Jonah did. But if we know the truth and accept it, it will set us free. Free from independence from God, free from the worries that those around us face, free from the pressure of others' opinions about us, free from sin, FREEEEEEeeeeee.

EFFECT OF DEPENDENCE ON THOSE AROUND US

Interestingly, as we depend on God and His miracles for our deliverance, it not only affects our relationship with Him; it also shows God's providence to all of those around. Think of how the Canaanites knew of the Hebrews and their God because of their miraculous deliverance from Egypt. They heard what happened to Pharaoh's army and were terrified of a God that might do the same thing to them!

This point was pressed home to me when I was reading David's response to Goliath when they met on the battlefield. David had just picked up his stones when Goliath said to him, "'Am I a dog, that you come at me with sticks?'. . . David said to the Philistine, 'You come against me with sword and spear and javelin, but I come against you in the name of the Lord Almighty, the God of the armies of Israel, whom you have defied. This day the Lord will deliver you into my hands, and I'll strike you down. . . . *And the whole world will know that there is a God in Israel. All those gathered here will know that it is not by sword or spear that the Lord saves; for the battle is the Lord's, and he will give all of you into our hands'*" (1 Sam. 17:43-47).

In other words, David relayed that the Lord was going to deliver Goliath into his hand so that all would know His power. Don't you think this is what the Lord wants from each of us? To depend on Him fully? Through the things that He does for and through us, He shows everyone around us His character and sovereignty. Not just in small things, but slaying proverbial giants that could not even be touched without His hand.

But first He must have our dependence on Him or we will never be victorious over any giants. If we remain in the safety of our normal spheres and comfort zones, He cannot show His power and might.

I had just finished speaking about dependence on God with a group of campers and my son and I headed back to our tent. We had traveled light, and I had brought a space- and weight-conscious "mummy-style" sleeping bag. Previously it had caused me severe claustrophobia because I couldn't adequately move my legs around in it, but I thought I would be fine this time inasmuch as the weather was to be warmer and I could sleep with the bag open, letting my legs have more room. I was thankful that the first few nights had been warm, so sleeping on top of the bag worked great.

Unfortunately, this night was different. It was chilly by the campfire, so I knew it was going to be cold away from it! I would be freezing if I didn't zip up the sleeping bag, but the thought of it made me cringe (a feeling you fellow claustrophobics will recognize).

I had just talked about Philippians 4:6, 7: "Do not be anxious about anything, but in every situation, by prayer and petition, with thanksgiving, present your requests to God. And the peace of God, which transcends all understanding, will guard your hearts and your minds in Christ Jesus."

In the midst of my anxiety the Holy Spirit asked me, "Do you really believe that you shouldn't be anxious about anything? Aren't you anxious right now?" I had to agree, I was definitely anxious, but I was not presenting my problem to God. Right then and there, I stopped and said, *Lord, I know You can take this away from me; please do.* I got into my sleeping bag, zipped up the sides, and with two additional prayers for momentary relapses of anxiety, had complete peace and great sleep. The cold weather continued for several nights and God remained true to His word of giving me peace.

These are the types of victories in Him that may not seem that huge a deal when we look back at them, but at the time they feel major. Jesus wants us to depend fully on Him so that we can see these victories in our lives on a daily basis as He gives us the abundant life that He promised (John 10:10).

Unfortunately, as I look back on times when I faced a "giant" in my life, faced it on my own and failed, I wonder what would have happened to those around me if I had truly faced the situation through dependence. If I had humbly submitted to the knowledge that God was growing me or someone else through the situation, would my family, friends, or acquaintances have seen the power of God as I faced that mountain in my life that appeared so unconquerable?

Would they have been encouraged to meet their "giants" through Him because of my success through God's intervention? How many times have I turned others away from God by my independence and subsequent obvious lack of power in my life? If others note the successes and recognize God's working, they will also notice the failures.

Interestingly, though, as we conquer the small foes through Him, He gives us the confidence that He can help us conquer the bigger and harder things in our lives. As the dependence grows, He challenges us to allow Him to work with us in slaying those "giants," giving those around us even more evidence of His working in our lives.

DEPENDENCE LEADS TO PRAISE

When we humbly submit to God and He gives us victories such as David had with Goliath—or on a much smaller scale, such as I had with claustrophobia—our natural response is heartfelt praise. "I will praise your name, Lord, for it is good. You have delivered me from all my troubles" (Ps. 54:6, 7).

"You, God, are my God, earnestly I seek you; I thirst for you, my whole being longs for you, in a dry and parched land where there is no water. I have seen you in the sanctuary and beheld your power and your glory.

Because your love is better than life, my lips will glorify you. I will praise you as long as I live, and in your name I will lift up my hands. I will be fully satisfied as with the richest of foods; with singing lips my mouth will praise you. . . . Because you are my help, I sing in the shadow of your wings. I cling to you; your right hand upholds me" (Ps. 63:1-8).

Just as food for the hungry or water for the thirsty leads to satisfaction, God's protection and guidance of His dependents leads to praise. It is a natural relationship. I am protected and preserved out of no goodness of my own; I respond with praise because I have been protected and cared for through His unfailing kindness and mercy. It wasn't until I had experienced the care and protection of God through dependence that I was able to understand the depth of emotion that David had when he wrote his psalms of praise. Thankfulness and praise follow an experiential knowledge of His guardianship.

PRAISE IN ADVERSITY

What? Praise in adversity?

This is when our dependence and our resolve to stay true to our sovereign King are tested the most vigorously. We see that things around us do not look optimistic, but we praise Him anyway because we know that even though on the surface things don't look good, whatever happens will be to His glory and will ultimately bring about His good, which will finally bring about the best for our good. Thus, we can praise Him even when the outcomes do not look good and there aren't good things happening. Remember Paul and Silas in jail, after being beaten, singing praises to God? I am sure that on a human level, things couldn't have looked much bleaker. But they knew the God behind the scenes!

When one is able to praise God in the middle of adversity there is an extra measure of energy available for dealing with the adversity. I have noted this most definitely when I have been training. When I am physically hurting at the end of an endurance event or training for one, if I think of or am willing to praise God for His help and for helping me to get to the point I am at, I have a burst of energy that lasts as long as I continue to praise Him. It is quite incredible.

CHAPTER 13

IS OUR DIRECTION ALTERED BY DEPENDENCE?

DEPENDENCE AND SURETY OF DIRECTION

A person's steps are directed by the Lord. How then can anyone understand their own way?" (Prov. 20:24).

When we are living in a state of dependence on God, are we *more* or *less* sure of our direction? Are we assured of what is going to happen today or tomorrow? What was it like for the children of Israel on their trip from Egypt? Did they have control over when they traveled or rested, gathered food, or watered their animals?

When the cloud moved, they packed and left. When the cloud stopped, the congregation stopped and set up camp. Water was obtained when God made it available. Manna was collected in the morning and not held over except on Fridays. They really had very little control over what was going to happen the rest of this day, let alone the next day.

Each could respond to this in the flesh and feel irritation with God for His wanting to control everything. On the other hand, it could feel very comfortable not to have to worry about necessities. Though the environment was not exactly peaceful because of a lack of resources, potential encounters with wild animals or venomous reptiles, as well as the constant threat of attack from unfriendly desert inhabitants, His guiding hand would protect and lead through all situations for the good of each individual in the camp.

They could view it as "there was no room for self-expression or individuality," or it could look like a wonderful thing, hiding under the wings of the Almighty. The latter type of full submission is what He wanted of them even after they arrived in the Promised Land, and it's what He wants from us today.

Unfortunately, the Israelites didn't like the unexpected or the waiting on God's timing. Though in Egypt they had been slaves, at least they knew what the next day held for them. They knew what their diet would consist of and what they would be doing. When God was in control of their days, there was just too much uncertainty. This likely contributed to the reason they kept asking to go back to their old lives in Egypt.

When I am in control of my schedule, priorities, and plans, things are pretty well laid out and some even set in concrete. On the other hand, when my will is submitted to God and He is leading my life on a moment-to-moment basis, my plans and schedule are no longer my own. God's will and ideal for my life are the priority, so the pressure to accomplish a goal by a certain time takes a backseat. I am less sure of my predetermined schedule and much less sure of my plans for the future.

Recently I have experienced the cultural pressures of maintaining independence in my own life. As I have noted before, I do orthopedic trauma. In 2007 I was impressed that I should leave classic orthopedics and work in an independent ministry, setting up a spiritual retreat. I would practice as a fill-in orthopedic surgeon (locum tenens) to provide financially for my family as well as maintain my surgical skills.

Several providential occurrences assured me that I was in the position the Lord wanted me in—a state of dependence on my part. Since that decision, many conversations with family, friends, and acquaintances drift to my plans for the future and when will I go back to a *regular* job. If I'm in a state of true dependence, I can't really give a clear answer to those questions. But, whether intentionally or not, those types of questions can push me outside of that dependent relationship that God wants me to have. I can begin questioning whether I'm achieving what I had in mind for my life instead of focusing on what God's plans are for me.

Though I believe God wants us to be scheduled and very committed to making the most of our time, He doesn't want us to make self-determined to-do lists more important than those around us who are in need. This point was brought home to me in the midst of a very busy clinic. I had been running behind schedule the whole morning. I was examining a hip-fracture patient and removing her surgical staples. It came out during our conversation that her husband had recently been diagnosed with terminal lung cancer. I was impressed to slow down and listen to her struggles and concerns.

As we finished the conversation I offered to pray with her about her husband's condition, which she quickly accepted. We prayed and continued to share our walk with God on each subsequent visit. After her husband died she told me that she treasured those times of sharing and prayer. Even though listening to her put me significantly behind in my schedule, the relationship we developed was significant for me and was what God was influencing me to do.

For us to be fully committed to Him we must be willing and eager to accept the variations in our schedule and life plans as He leads us. We will be less sure of the direction we are going or what tomorrow or even next year holds, but we are confident in our Leader; in that faith we peacefully progress through whatever He has in store for us. Psalm 119:105 reminds us that "[God's] word is a lamp for my feet, a light on my path." It doesn't mention a beacon into the future, just a simple light on the path that we are walking, maybe only a step or two ahead.

James 4:13-17 talks about how we make plans independent of God and then boastfully say that we will do this or that tomorrow. We will go to this city, or next year do something else. James advises that we should acknowledge these as *our* plans, to be done only if it is God's will. Placing our dependence on Him in all areas is critical.

" 'Woe to the obstinate children,' declares the Lord, 'to those who carry out plans that are not mine' " (Isa. 30:1). "Why, you do not even know what will happen tomorrow. What is your life? You are a mist that appears for a little while and then vanishes" (James 4:14).

ENTERING THE "WILDERNESS"

"Many look back to the Israelites, and marvel at their unbelief and murmuring, feeling that they themselves would not have been so ungrateful; but when their faith is tested, even by little trials, they manifest no more faith or patience than did ancient Israel. When brought into strait places, they murmur at the process by which God has chosen to purify them. Though their present needs are supplied, many are unwilling to trust God for the future, and they are in constant anxiety lest poverty shall come upon them, and their children shall be left to suffer. Some are always anticipating evil or magnifying the difficulties that really exist, so that their eyes are blinded to the many blessings which demand their gratitude. The obstacles they encounter, instead of leading them to seek help from God, the only Source of strength, separate them from Him, because they awaken unrest and repining" (*Patriarchs and Prophets,* pp. 293, 294).

What will the trials you face do to you? It all depends on the condition of your heart. The trials can either lead us to depend on God in a more significant way, purifying our hearts as we see the trials as gifts from

Him; or they can separate us from Him "because they awaken unrest and repining." It all depends on the condition of the heart!

Unfortunately, I relate well with the children of Israel. I recently had a week when I had a lot of things to get done and everything seemed to go wrong. It was tax return week, and I was doing my kids' returns. In addition, I was getting paperwork together for a hospital that I was going to go to in the near future, and trying to organize programs and construction work at the New Beginnings Ranch. I had to prepare to teach an anatomy lab, do preparation for my son's homeschool Bible class, and take care of a charity health clinic.

That was all OK, but as the week progressed, problems began to crop up. Unappreciative attitudes were hurled my way. Seemingly irresolvable issues came up, despite many attempts to settle them. What had happened to me? Initially, things were fine. I held on to my hope and maintained a peaceful attitude. But then as the problems mushroomed I started feeling sorry for myself.

Things went only downhill from there. My fuse got short, and it took only a little provocation to set me off. Aggressive words were shared with those responsible for the irresolvable issues. Overall, I experienced a true separation from God because of my self-pity and the complaining that resulted.

I had entered the wilderness with the children of Israel. Jesus went to the wilderness to be tempted. We enter the wilderness because of temptations, hurts, falls, failures, questioning, or just waiting. Sometimes it is from the circumstances we are in, and sometimes we go there voluntarily.

We are always tempted in the wilderness. Tempted to give up. Find another way. Doubt the Giver. Doubt our experience. Doubt our conversion. Doubt our resolve. The devil comes and gives us the "if" questions he gave to Christ, though perhaps in a different format.

- *If you are really changed, why . . .*
- *If you were truly dependent on God, then you wouldn't . . .*
- *It would be easier if you just gave up on trying to depend on God. Why not try this . . .*

Max Lucado reminds us, when in the wilderness, not to "doubt the Giver, but to doubt the doubts" (*Next Door Savior, Wilderness Places*, pp. 117-121). Allow yourself to see that even though things are not as you would like, God will work out something good to come from the situation.

DEPENDENCE AND OUTCOMES OF SITUATIONS

"Rejoice always, pray continually, give thanks in all circumstances; for this is God's will for you in Christ Jesus" (1 Thess. 5:16-18). This text can be understood and followed only in the context of dependence. It would seem impossible to give thanks when you have a family member who has been diagnosed with terminal cancer, or your spouse has left you, or your children have left the morals of their upbringing, or a host of other circumstances. The only way one could follow this command is through complete dependence on His sovereignty. Anything less than that would result in fear, anxiety, and self-pity.

On Parent's Weekend at Union College, I accompanied my oldest daughter, Kari, to "Gear Room" lesson study. "Gear Room" is a group of young adults known for their potentially eccentric ways of making spiritual points. On this particular day we were to participate in a "trust fall." When my turn came I was blindfolded and helped up onto a chair. I was told I could fall back at any time because the others were ready to catch me. I fell back, but no one caught me! Instead I landed on a very soft mattress, unhurt, but somewhat incensed that I hadn't felt someone catching me as I fell.

I then stepped back mentally to look at the situation from the big picture. There had been people who would make sure that I would not miss the mattress when I fell. And I had a soft landing, possibly more comfortable than being caught by a number of arms. Actually, looking back, it was a better way to land than what I had expected.

The spiritual lesson was that sometimes God doesn't always catch us the way we expect. Yes, we are fine after the fall, and when we are honest with ourselves we can admit that we landed in a better way than we had expected. But sometimes we are incensed with God's audacity to go outside of our expectations and prayerful wishes.

Putting our dependence on God doesn't always result in our desired outcome. It was my wife's birthday, and she set out to have an enjoyable ride on her favorite horse, Doc. He was not only her favorite horse but the horse she had always wanted—one that craved her attention and love, then responded by trying to please. When she was riding him that day, it was obvious something was wrong. His normally precise foot placement when trotting over logs was clumsy, and when she got off of him and he headed down the hill he was hardly able to walk upright.

We prayerfully submitted Doc's situation to the Lord and asked for

His guidance; I felt sure He was going to heal Doc for His glory. We had several vet evaluations, but it became increasingly apparent that this was a degenerative problem in the vertebrae of the neck, which was putting pressure on his nerves and producing instability in his legs.

We tried all the recommended procedures, with no improvement. The upshot was that Doc didn't know where his feet were and was having a difficult time with his balance. At any time he could fall over and hurt himself or whoever was working with him. We were absolutely crushed that there was nothing else we could do. The vet felt we should put him down because of the safety issues.

"Where are You, God?" I cried out. "I know You can take care of this!" I was sure that He was going to heal Doc because of how special he was to us and because God had blessed our family through him. But alas, it was over.

Shortly after we had Doc put down, my youngest (age 12 at the time) told my wife, "Mom, I might not have learned to trust God if it hadn't been for this situation with Doc." Though we didn't get the outcome we had prayed for, my daughter had learned to trust Him. Was there still a sense of loss? Yes. Would we have changed anything in exchange for the lesson in trust that she learned? Never!

Even when we do not understand, an answer will come, sometimes here on earth, sometimes not until we are in heaven. But we live by faith, in a submitted stance.

There was a family in which controversy between various members and estrangement from one another resulted in turmoil. Then the mother was diagnosed with cancer, which had progressed significantly. Prayers and petitions were lifted to God in all earnestness and humility, but no healing occurred. Instead she was laid to rest in Jesus.

"If I am depending on You, Jesus, aren't You going to take care of me and those things that are important to me?" is often the question on our minds in such a situation. The answer is "Yes," not always how we want but how He sees fit. Oh, by the way, the family of the woman who died of cancer resolved their conflicts; there was an awakening of the importance of God in their lives. Do you think that the dying woman would have traded her life so that the familial estrangement was cleared and the family members could find a walk with Jesus? Yes! Some things are more important than life to us—such as the eternal outcome of those we love, for one.

In a similar way God sees that death is not the worst thing that can happen to us. Our first death is, to God, but a mere comma in our existence with Him. He will do almost anything to get through to us and help us to avoid the second death. That is what He wants each of us to avoid. He never wastes our pain. There is a reason for everything, though we may not understand it in this life.

When I think of unfair circumstances in the Bible, I'm reminded of three incidents:

- Jesus and how He deserved none of the pain and suffering, estrangement from His Father, or bearing our sins.
- Job losing everything, including his children and health, then never getting a response from God as to why it happened.
- Ezekiel, as an object lesson to Israel, losing his wife a day after it was prophesied and then being told not to mourn over her loss.

Dan Allender, in speaking about the unfair treatment of Christ (*NIV Men's Devotional Bible,* p. 766), says:

"The Servant of God understood that faith was not a protective shield against the brutality of those who beat Him or the ignominy of those who pulled out His beard. . . . Nevertheless, no one could stand as His accuser and bring His soul to shame because the Father stood as His advocate and judge. . . . For most, trusting God means relying on Him to keep our body or our world intact. But that is not Biblical trust at its essential core. Trust involves relying on Him for what is most essential to our being: the intactness of our soul. A return to the Father ensures that no one can shame or disgrace or possess our soul . . . no matter what is done to our body, reputation or temporal security."

Dependence on God may not always lead to a good outcome by our standard, until we see the bigger picture. Unfortunately, many times we cannot see the bigger picture here on earth and will have to wait for heaven to understand the "why."

DEPENDENTLY WAITING

Max Lucado shares a family experience of boarding an airplane.

"When I travel with my kids, I carry all our tickets in my satchel. When the moment comes to board the plane, I stand between the attendant and the child. As each daughter passes, I place a ticket in her hand. She, in turn, gives the ticket to the attendant. Each one receives the ticket in the nick of time. What I do for my daughters God does for you. He places himself between you and the need. And at the right time, he gives you the ticket" (*Traveling Light,* p. 49).

My own experience of getting what I needed from God at the right time, not a moment too soon or too late, has been repeated again and again in my life. Often when a strategy seems completely set, something happens at the last minute that changes the planned course. It is usually in a providential way, making it obvious He has been working to accomplish the goal.

When I quit classic orthopedics and went to a "fill-in" type of practice (locum tenens), I planned to work at a level-one trauma center in Georgia for four days every three weeks. With my Georgia license and a schedule planned all the way from September through December, I was set.

A week and a half before going for my first assignment I received a phone call that my services were not needed. My family is in the habit of eating and we like to stay current on our utility bills, so I became just a little nervous! "Lord, we have a problem here," I prayed. That morning I called a friend in western Nebraska, knowing there had been a need in the past to help cover the hospital's orthopedics. He confirmed there was still a need and put me in contact with the woman in charge of scheduling physician coverage.

As I queried about the opening, she said, "Yes, and just this morning the orthopedic surgeon covering for September called and canceled." I checked my schedule with theirs, and the exact dates I had been canceled for work in Georgia were when I was needed in Nebraska! I wondered in amazement at the exactness of God's timing and assignment. "The Lord is good to those who wait for him, to the soul that seeks him. It is good that one should wait quietly for the salvation of the Lord" (Lam. 3:25, 26, RSV).

Following God's directions to our Promised Land requires faith and a willingness to wait upon God and His timing.

"Those who wait for me will not be put to shame" (Isa. 49:23, RSV).

"Wait for the Lord, and keep to his way, and he will exalt you" (Ps. 37:34, RSV).

I discovered a new meaning to "waiting on the Lord" after running 10.25 miles several years ago (and other times since). When I started the run and several times during it, I wasn't sure I had enough stamina to get through the whole course. I found, as I was running, that it was important for me to concentrate on the present, not on the future. I was to wait on the Lord for strength; when I reached the portion of the run where I needed strength, the Lord would give it to me, not when I didn't need it. "Wait for the Lord; be strong and take heart and wait for the Lord" (Ps. 27:14).

When we wait patiently for God, we do so because we have a dependent trust in His ability to give us what we need when we need it. With this kind of trusting relationship with Him we can be assured that we will not be put to shame. He promises that He will exalt us and renew our strength.

MEN AND DEPENDENCE

Why is it that there is a preponderance of women involved in God-centered activities? Is it because men are so busy providing for the family? Maybe, but I think it goes much deeper.

"The modern 'macho' man in American society is not supposed to be vulnerable. According to research, the five most difficult statements for the modern man to make are (1) I don't know; (2) I was wrong; (3) I need help; (4) I'm afraid; and (5) I'm sorry. In other words, according to the world's definition, real men do not admit any vulnerability. And if they do, their masculinity is in question" (D. Stuart Briscoe, *NIV Men's Devotional Bible*, p. 1132).

Perhaps men do not want to be seen as vulnerable or dependent on anything, including God. Men often think that women are supposed to be vulnerable and dependent on something outside of themselves, but not men.

How do we decide to order our lives overall? Usually we either settle for the pursuit of possessions (the rat race) or that of relationships (God, family, friends).

"The way in which we measure our standard of living indicates the race we have decided to run. . . . We can choose the rat race, or we can choose to not love this world and 'throw off everything that hinders and the sin that so easily entangles, and . . . run with perseverance the race marked out for us' (Hebrews 12:1)" (*NIV Men's Devotional Bible*, p. 1192).

Are we going to continue in the rat race, hanging on to its "treasures" while losing important relationships with friends, family, and even God? Is clinging to our "standard of living" more important?

Our decisions and leadership in this arena are so important! The devil knows who in the family to attack to most effectively destroy the family unit and subdue its effectiveness.

Steve Farrar writes: "The enemy is no fool. He has a strategically designed game plan, a diabolical method he employs time and time again. When he wants to destroy a family, he focuses on the man. For if he can neutralize the man . . . he has neutralized the family. And the damage that takes place when a man's family leadership is neutralized is beyond calculation" (*NIV Men's Devotional Bible*, p. 1361).

Men, God is calling us to dependence as well. He doesn't want us to depend on others, the government, financial-aid packages, handouts, or anything else here in this world. He wants us to provide for our families and take care of our responsibilities. But He wants us to do it in His strength and always through His direction.

World Series Most Valuable Player award winner Orel Hershiser states it this way:

"It's my faith that lifts me up when I've failed. It's my faith that reminds me of my true insignificance when the world has been laid at my feet because of my success throwing a ball. To call myself a Christian and then not strive to be the best I can be and do the most I can with what has been given me would be the height of hypocrisy. Being a Christian is no excuse for mediocrity or passive acceptance of defeat. If anything, Christianity demands a higher standard, more devotion for the task" (*NIV Men's Devotional Bible*, p. 1312).

Thus, our faith (dependence on God) makes us more eager for the tasks God gives us and raises the standard we strive to reach through His strength. Our dependence also smoothes out the ups and downs—humility in success (it is not our triumph, but God's), and growth in tribulation.

God desires men who are willing to step away from being a "world's man" to becoming a humble, vulnerable man who leads his family toward a faith/trust in God: the true anchor of the soul and the family. The thought of men such as this leaves the devil shaking in his boots.

CHAPTER 14

ARE DEPENDENCE AND FAITH RELATED?

DEPENDENCE AND FAITH

Recently I was criticized for making dependence more important than faith in the Christian walk, which if true would have been a valid criticism. One needs to step back and look at the definition of dependence: (1) humbly understanding that we need a Savior; (2) realizing that Jesus is our sovereign Creator and Savior; (3) submitting to His will in each moment; (4) keeping the two-way communication intact throughout the day. Then compare these characteristics with those of the giants of faith in Hebrews 11.

In each case the faith hero exhibited the qualities of dependence in their actions. Abraham depended on God when he left his home to go to a foreign land, unknown and untried. He depended on God when he lifted up the knife to sacrifice Isaac, knowing God could bring about His promise of a great nation some other way if He chose. Dependence on God is what the faith chapter is all about!

In the past I thought of faith as an active trust or deep belief. That is true, but true dependence goes so much deeper than the old definition I had. Now I hesitate even to describe dependence as "faith," since it tends to lose its distinctiveness because of my formerly inadequate definition.

"Now faith is confidence in what we hope for and assurance about what we do not see. . . . And without faith it is impossible to please God, because anyone who comes to him must believe that he exists and that he rewards those who earnestly seek him" (Heb. 11:1-6).

This is the description of faith, and the remainder of Hebrews 11 is devoted to revealing how faith/dependence is demonstrated in the life of a faith hero. There is always an action taken as a response to a prompting by God.

Many define faith as belief or trust. The problem with such a definition is that it can be adhered to without any change in one's life. We are told that "even the demons believe that—and shudder" (James 2:19). Trust is good, but it doesn't mean that one is going to be radically altered by engaging in it. I trust my children driving, but when it is icy outside I still worry over their safety. I can trust an employee to work for me, but will I trust him with my checkbook and all my assets? Can I depend on him to take care of all of the details of my business?

Trust has multiple levels of commitment. One can opt for a limited trust model for their faith, but that could deprive them of the larger blessings and peace that accompany the dependence I've described. Trust can be given, but there may be an element of worry associated with that trust. As mentioned earlier, one can have trust or belief without the humility that is crucial to true dependence. Faith has to be so much more than just trust. Thus, I believe when God talks about faith He's speaking of dependence.

Let's look at a few texts that discuss faith and see if dependence fits. "Take up the shield of faith, with which you can extinguish all the flaming darts of the evil one" (Eph. 6:16). Replace "faith" with "dependence" leading to quenching all the flaming darts of the evil one.

Is there any other method of quenching the flaming arrows of the devil than dependence? My humble acceptance that I cannot do it on my own prods me to rely fully on Jesus, giving me the right response to the flaming dart. I then submit to His will. "Submit yourselves, then, to God. Resist the devil, and he will flee from you. Come near to God and he will come near to you" (James 4:7, 8)

"The righteous person shall live by his faithfulness" (Hab. 2:4). The righteous shall live by their "dependence"? Does this fit if I am talking about the humble understanding of my need for a Savior, acceptance of Jesus as that sovereign Creator-Savior, submitting to His will and listening for His voice? The thought of righteousness by dependent faith gives a different slant on the subject. We know that anything we *do* does not make us more acceptable to God, and only our faith (or dependence) saves us through His grace. Interestingly, if we try to become right with God it is done out of independence, which is nothing more than sin! If everything is done out of dependence, we are operating only through *His* strength and direction, exactly how He planned we should live.

Second Corinthians 5:7: "We live by faith, not by sight." Or, we live by "dependence," not by sight. Again, our dependence *is* our sight as we depend on Jesus to make the way for us outside of our human preconceptions of thinking "inside the box." The Holy Spirit makes our way visible as the lamp for our feet and the light on our path. We obtain our moment-by-moment direction from His guiding our way. Often (maybe usually) that guidance doesn't lead us where we think we are going, but often out of our comfort zone and into the areas that we never thought we would enter.

Let's try another. "Everything that does not come from faith is sin" (Rom. 14:23). Or, whatever does not proceed from dependence is sin. Anything done independently is sin if we're trying to live life outside of God's leading. Let's face it—every sin that we commit happens when we lose a dependent hold on God. When my son and I have an argument or disagreement, I can respond in the flesh and angrily deal with his lack of respect or inability to appropriately resolve conflict. This results in our separation from each other as well as my own separation from God and His will for me. On the other hand, if I will respond in a God-dependent manner I am able to see the situation, not as an attack on my authority or fatherhood, but as an opportunity that God allowed for either my or my son's growth. I can then ask the Lord for His guidance in preventing any separation between us. In the Spirit I can respond and maintain my relationship with both my son and God.

Try using "dependence" in any of the Bible texts that refer to faith and see if the correlation holds true. From my experience, it always does. This has brought a whole new depth to my faith and understanding of how God wants to change me into His new creation. New life in Him comes about, not by my effort but simply by asking God for a dependent spirit and making choices that will keep me in that state of humble dependence.

Many Christians are unwilling to go to the depths of dependence in their walk with Jesus. The youth see a problem with the powerless religion they observe and they do not want to be a part of it. They need the examples of their parents and other Christians showing dependence on God. With something so counterculture as dependence, it's powerful to observe what it looks like in someone's life. Even with this visual, the opinions of others and temptations of independence can make maintaining the connection a difficult task.

HOUSE BUILT ON THE ROCK

In Luke 6:48, 49 Jesus speaks of two houses, one built on rock and the other built on sand. Of course Jesus is the Rock we are to build our lives on, and the sand is anything else that we might choose as more important than Christ. I believe that Jesus is again talking about full dependence on

Him. How could we be more fully anchored to Him than living in a truly dependent relationship? When the winds of strife blow, when the floods of error threaten to wash us away, if we are firmly held by complete reliance on Him, nothing can topple us.

Granted, it can take a long time to build this type of "house." It doesn't go up overnight like one built on independent desires and plans. But the prolonged, painstaking, comfort-stretching work is worthwhile when the storms come and we remain calm because we know the strength of the foundation Rock.

An important key is to be anchored in the most foundational part of your life—at the core of your very existence, the part from where all your dreams and aspirations arise, where your true identity comes from. When this is truly submitted to Christ on a continual basis, with the knowledge of both your need and the acceptance of Christ as your sovereign Savior, your house will be built on the foundation Rock. Any portion of independence from that Rock-solid foundation could place you on shifting sand, which will not withstand the storms of life. This dependence is the only type of protection that will bring us through the final time of Jacob's trouble. In the end we will not be able to rely on our wealth, family, friends, good job, or anything else outside of our Rock of salvation.

As mentioned earlier, this type of foundation is not built overnight. It can take years of trial and error, experimenting with Jesus and finding out which voice in our heart is truly His. It requires learning, sometimes painfully, that our way can lead down roads we wish we hadn't taken. It takes years or decades of resubmitting our thoughts, dreams, and even our identities, learning not to worry about the approval of others but focusing only on Him who has commissioned us.

RIGHTEOUSNESS BY FAITH

This is so important we have to revisit this, in addition to that listed in the dependence and faith section. We mentioned Habakkuk 2:4: "The righteous person will live by his faithfulness." This same thought is borne out in Romans 1:17, Galatians 3:11, and Hebrews 10:38, 39. Jesus also talks about this in His parable of the wedding feast, in which each individual was given a wedding garment. The covering robe of Christ's righteousness, or righteousness by faith, is the subject.

"When the king came in to view the guests, the real character of all was revealed. For every guest at the feast there had been provided a wedding garment. This garment was a gift from the king. By wearing it the guests showed their respect for the giver of the feast. But one man was clothed in his common citizen dress. He had refused to make the preparation required by the king. The garment provided for him at great cost he disdained to wear. . . . It is the righteousness of Christ, His own unblemished character, that through faith is imparted to all who receive Him as their personal Saviour. . . . This robe, woven in the loom of heaven, has in it not one thread of human devising" (*Christ's Object Lessons*, pp. 309-311).

If this robe has nothing to do with human devising and if it is given to us as Christ's own unblemished character, this must be dealing with dependence, wherein we are humbly listening and submitting to His sovereignty in our life and the universe.

In Eden Adam and Eve lost their righteousness. It happened when they "severed their connection with God, and the light that had encircled them departed. Naked and ashamed, they tried to supply the place of the heavenly garments by sewing together fig leaves for a covering" (*ibid.*, p. 310).

Whenever the connection with God is lost we try to manage things on our own. We try to create our own righteousness by keeping the Sabbath better, having a diet that is more vegan, or a variety of other ideas. We feel that if we do all this great stuff, our acceptance by Jesus is more certain than that of the sinners down the street. After all, we are serious about doing the right thing and work at it harder than anyone else. Surely there will be some reward for that, we reason. "God, You really need to recognize my successful efforts as better than those of the people around me (maybe even above the accomplishments and sacrifice of Your Son!)."

CHAPTER 15

WHAT IS KEEPING
YOU FROM DEPENDING?

It was late, and I was eager to get home. My flight had been delayed, and now it appeared the pilot had taken off to the west while home was due east! Two, three, maybe four minutes went by as I waited for the plane to bank and turn back. *"What is this pilot thinking? I want to get home!"* I raged. Almost frantically I peered out my tiny airplane window, searching in all directions until I finally spotted the lights of Denver to the rear. We had been heading in the right direction the entire time!

I sat in the cramped airplane seat and mulled over the past few moments. Thinking I had the directions figured out, I actually had only a small airplane-window view of my surroundings. The pilot not only had a better view but all the latest technology to show him where to go.

My egocentric idea that I knew which direction to go with the plane is not new to the human condition. During the entire Exodus the Israelites repeatedly questioned God's provision and leading. They had been given an amazing promise from the God of the universe. If they would depend on Him, they were promised that they would not have to worry about anything—food, water, shelter, clothing, or anything else they needed. Though their journey from Egypt was one of learning dependence, many of them never reached a state of dependence or even the Promised Land.

Let's look back at the underlying reasons for their failures to reach dependence. We may even catch a glimpse of ourselves along that same journey through the desert.

Early in the journey the devil successfully used difficult circumstances to derail the chosen ones from a course of depending on God. Whether the Red Sea in front of them and Pharaoh's army behind, trying to slake their thirst with bitter water at Marah, or the ever-looming question of whether they would have food tomorrow (or even today), the short-sighted Hebrews always seemed to have abundant reason to question why they were in the desert rather than back in Egypt. They were basically telling God, "You are not big enough for this problem, so we'd prefer to be slaves in the hands of the Egyptians where life was at least a little more certain."

Days after the wonderful and powerful demonstration of God's power at Sinai, the people convinced Aaron to make a golden calf for them. Exodus 32:5, 6 states, "Aaron made proclamation and said, 'Tomorrow shall be a feast to the Lord.' And they rose up early on the morrow, and offered burnt offerings and brought peace offerings; and the people sat down to eat and drink, and rose up to play" (RSV).

Do you think they truly planned to have a feast to the Lord? Yes, it was a feast and yes, it was to something they treated as lord, but it was not to *the* Lord. I believe the problem here is similar to what Cain experienced (see Gen. 4:3-6). There was worship going on, but in a manner that was not honoring God in humble obedience. There was worship, but it was of the created and not of the Creator. It was worship of what *they* had done and not what God had done. The people thought only about what pleased them, without regard for what was pleasing to God. I would define this as independence, not anywhere near the dependence God desired from them.

Numbers 11 records how the people were complaining about their many misfortunes, including the lack of meat for them to eat. They were being completely cared for, and yet they were not satisfied. They wanted their perverted appetites satisfied, and they wanted God to provide meat now!

Aaron and Miriam were not exempt from joining in the fray. Racial bigotry, desire for personal recognition, and speaking out against God's appointed leader proved to be their testing (and failing) ground. They spoke out against Moses because his wife was from another nation, and they said, "Has the Lord indeed spoken only through Moses? Has He not spoken through us also?"

Probably the biggest test of Israel's dependence on God was the return of the 12 spies from Canaan. The Israelites had two opposing reports to choose from. Ten spies said, "The land, through which we have gone, to spy it out, is a land that devours its inhabitants; and all the people that we saw in it are men of great stature. . . . And we seemed to ourselves like grasshoppers, and so we seemed to them" (Num. 13:32, 33, RSV).

Caleb and Joshua gave quite a different report: "Let us go up at once, and occupy it; for we are well able to overcome it" (verse 30, RSV). "If the Lord delights in us, he will bring us into this land and give it to us, a land which flows with milk and honey. Only, do not rebel against the Lord; and do not fear the people of the land, for they are bread for us; their protection is removed from them, and the Lord is with us; do not fear them" (Num. 14:8, 9, RSV).

Unfortunately, almost all the adults of Israel sided with the 10 in their independence from God, making them unfit for entrance into the Promised Land. In the shadow of the giants they could not see past the behemoths to the God whose power dwarfed them.

Interestingly and tragically, after being told that they could not enter Canaan but must die in the wilderness for their unbelief (or independence), the people changed their minds and decided to fight the Canaanites. Again they were acting independently of God. However, God had withdrawn His power because of their lack of faith, and they were routed in defeat. Sullenly they returned to the wilderness, as God had instructed, not in a spirit of repentance for their disobedience but because they were out of options.

The desire for self-exaltation and autonomy was demonstrated in the revolt of Korah, Dathan, and Abiram (see Num. 16). The subsequent judgment, when the earth swallowed up all the families of those in rebellion, only brought further grumbling.

"But on the morrow all the congregation of the people of Israel murmured against Moses and against Aaron, saying, 'You have killed the people of the Lord'" (verse 41, RSV).

They failed to see that God was the one in control, not Moses.

The last of their departures from dependence on God is probably the most heart-wrenching. Moses, after dealing with these wayward people and putting up with their complaining—on a number of occasions pleading with God to spare them—gave in to independence. Numbers 20:10-12 (RSV) records it like this:

"And he [Moses] said to them, 'Hear now, you rebels; shall we bring forth water for you out of this rock?' And Moses lifted up his hand and struck the rock with his rod twice; and water came forth abundantly, and the congregation drank, and their cattle. And the Lord said to Moses and Aaron, 'Because you did not believe in me, to sanctify me in the eyes of the people of Israel, therefore you shall not bring this assembly into the land which I have given them.'"

The difference between Moses' sin and that of most of the others was that Moses was willing to humbly repent and return to dependence. Though God fully forgave Moses, He did not remove the consequence of Moses' sin.

Numbers 22-25 records the incidents surrounding the request of the Midianites and Moabites for Balaam to curse the Hebrews. These tribes wanted to prevail against the formidable foe that had already destroyed many of their more powerful neighbors. But Balaam could speak only blessings instead of high-dollar curses, so they resorted to separating the children of Israel from God through idol worship and sexual licentiousness. Idolatry worked even better than curses, as many of the Israelites gave in to the sexual temptations and subsequent isolation from God. Only the complete removal (killing) of those who led the people astray stopped further separation from God.

After conquering Jericho, the children of Israel were to destroy everything except Rahab and her family. It was all to be burned, and the gold, silver, bronze, and iron were to be placed in the treasury of the Lord's house. Unfortunately, Achan's covetousness in keeping some of the spoils for himself resulted in the Israelites being defeated by the army of Ai and the ultimate stoning of Achan himself (see Joshua 7). Joshua forgot to consult with God before going to war, and this probably contributed to their defeat as well. The spies thought Ai would be an easy conquest. They sent fewer troops, but without God's blessing, these foes proved more than Israel could handle. Again, independence from God led to ruin and discouragement.

OUR REASONS FOR INDEPENDENCE FROM GOD

Do you find this account convicting? There is a lot to contemplate here! We are often faced with the same "giants" that caused the Hebrews and their leader to fail: self-exaltation, the need for personal recognition, covetousness, sexual gratification outside of the marriage covenant, taking credit that belongs only to God, and the influence of other people.

If we're honest we must admit to being plagued with the need for personal significance. As long as this need is satisfied within a dependent relationship with God, it is a good thing because it does not draw us away from God, family, and friends. But when it is not met within the framework that God had set in place, it is an ugly thing and will inevitably separate us from God, family, and friends.

RUN THE RACE

Paul likened the spiritual life to running a race: "I have fought the good fight, I have finished the race, I have kept the faith. Now there is in store

WHAT IS KEEPING YOU FROM DEPENDING?   103

for me the crown of righteousness, which the Lord, the righteous Judge, will award to me on that day—and not only to me, but also to all who have longed for his appearing" (2 Tim. 4:7, 8).

Yes, it took a lot to remain in Christ through faith, but in the end Paul could look back and say that he stayed on track, finished the race, and kept the faith. Struggle and effort? Yes! Worth it? Oh, yes!

We imagine we would never respond the way the Hebrews did in the wilderness, where their constant response to adversity consisted of finding fault in their leaders while wistfully thinking of how good life was back in Egypt. They did this in spite of much proof of God's guidance and providence. Are we really that different? When we meet problems beyond what we can deal with, do we remember God? Do we recall that it is God who is taking us on this journey to dependence on Him, or do we blame others for where we are? When we're successful, do we really place the glory in God's hands or do we say, "I did a really great job, so I must be a pretty cool person"? Do we really believe God is sovereign and that He is good? Is He honestly looking out for our best good?

Craig Groeschel writes about the Christian atheist, in *The Christian Atheist, Believing in God but Living as If He Doesn't Exist*. Stop and ponder what you claim to believe and how those beliefs are played out in your life. Are you a Christian atheist? Do you really believe that God is all-powerful and does not need your help in managing affairs, even if everything (humanly speaking) looks as though there is no way out of the situation, like the Hebrews on the edge of the Red Sea with Pharaoh and his army rapidly advancing? Does your walk reflect the talk?

Del Tackett asks if we are really satisfied with what God has offered us. God has given us everything we need, as He did for the Hebrews, but are we satisfied with that? It is similar to what God symbolized through Hosea and Gomer? Hosea provided everything for Gomer, including undeserved love, but what did Gomer do? She basically said, "Hosea, you are not enough for me," and then went out and prostituted herself with other lovers.

Will we go away from God to "prostitute" ourselves with the things of this world rather than stay with the One who truly loves us and has given everything we need?

As discussed earlier regarding "two-" versus "four-wheel" drive in the pickup, it is easier to choose the independent path in our daily lives. If we remain in full dependence on Jesus, we may experience exhaustion during and after trials. It may seem that we just can't go one step further in our dependent walk with Him. Jesus knew this when He gave John the revelator this message: "This calls for patient endurance on the part of the people of God who keep his commands and remain faithful [dependence] to Jesus" (Rev. 14:12).

This call is for the endurance of the saints. We are running a marathon and cannot be sidelined by lack of endurance or by lack of connection with our running Partner. Remember, He promises, "Those who hope in the Lord will renew their strength. . . . They will run and not grow weary" (Isa. 40:31).

"Therefore, since we are surrounded by such a great cloud of witnesses, let us throw off everything that hinders and the sin that so easily entangles. And let us run with perseverance the race marked out for us, fixing our eyes on Jesus, the pioneer and perfecter of faith" (Heb. 12:1, 2).

CLIMBING

It was my first day of aggressive rock climbing. We had warmed up on an easy route to get the feel of our climbing shoes as well as the use of a backup rope. I was ready to try climbing Cybernetics at Wall Street, near Moab, Utah. The young adults had already scaled the route unscathed for the most part. My ascent was not shaping up quite the same. There was a particularly steep section through which I was having a hard time maneuvering. I would progress up a handhold or two, then lose my grip and fall back to where I'd started—or even farther down. After recovering for a few seconds, I'd repeat the section, only to slide down again.

After this had happened at least five or six times, I started feeling as though I was holding up the other climbers and maybe I should quit. I wasn't even sure I was able to conquer that section of the wall. I expressed my concerns, but the cheering section below would not hear of it! I rested for a few more minutes, mustered all of my strength, used the handholds and sidewall to my advantage, and finished the climb successfully.

My ascending and falling back down reminded me of how this difficult section was similar to my Christian experience. I would go through certain events with great speed and ease, but then something that was particularly difficult would happen. I would try to get through the difficult section, but even when attempting it through His strength I would eventually lose my resolve and end up sliding back to where I'd been before, or even lower. Finally, after failing multiple times, I would resolve to keep my eyes on

Him throughout the entire trial and follow Him no matter what. Then and only then would I be able to get through the difficult section of life and continue on my spiritual climb to my ultimate destination.

CHAPTER 16

WHAT IS IMPORTANT IN YOUR LIFE?

Dependence on God allows us to slow down our busy lifestyles. We learn to stop the endless pursuit of others' approval based on our money, power, and prestige. We follow the call to "come apart with Me"; we find time in the midst of turmoil for communion with Him as He calls to us out of the pain. Dependence also allows us to have time with our families, specifically our spouses and children.

Most of us are so busy trying to make money in order to be independent that we don't have or take the time to be with our families. What is happening? We divorce as often as non-Christians; our children are rebelling (because their parents do not spend time with them). Yes, we do need to make a living so we are not depending on others or the government for food and shelter, but there is no need for the extras. We need time and margin for family and God. In order to have that extra time, we must trust God to know which things are essential and then discard everything else.

In contrast to the rich young ruler who was asked to give everything away, consider the widow with her two mites. It was not recorded that she was asked to give away everything she had, but Jesus said she did, and He praised her for it! Though she was the one who could have been the beneficiary of offerings and gifts inasmuch as she was a poor widow, she was giving everything for His service. What was the difference in the hearts of these two individuals? Self and monetary dependence reigned supreme for the rich young ruler; the widow had only complete dependence on God.

The condition of a dependent heart is what Jesus desires. He turned away the one who appeared, on the surface, most able to help His cause. On the other hand, He applauded the one with seemingly little to offer. Jesus remains committed to finding those with the right heart more than anything else. He can mold and make what He wants from the right heart, but a self-dependent spirit is not easily influenced.

"A person is not a Jew who is one only outwardly, nor is circumcision merely outward and physical. No, a person is a Jew who is one inwardly; and circumcision is circumcision of the heart, by the Spirit, not by the written code. Such a person's praise is not from other people, but from God" (Rom. 2:28, 29). A right heart, "circumcised" from the Spirit, is not worried about acceptance from anyone except God. Such a heart is willing to be led and taught, rather than be insistent on having its own way.

DEPENDENCE RETURNS US TO A TRUE IDENTITY

Interestingly, there is a spin-off of the dependence issue recorded in John 13:3, 4. It is a familiar story, but please do not miss the significance. Jesus had just come to the upper room with His disciples. The disciples had been selfishly vying for and arguing about which positions they would hold in the coming kingdom. No servant was available to wash the feet of the group.

"Jesus knew that the Father had put all things under his power, and that he had come from God and was returning to God; so he got up from the meal, took off his outer clothing, and wrapped a towel around his waist. After that, he poured water into a basin and began to wash his disciples' feet, drying them with the towel that was wrapped around him."

Something is wrong here! Disciples are to serve their master, not the other way around. This was the point Jesus was making. In a world of "doing it my way" or in a world of selfishly struggling to the top, disciples serve their masters, but in His government all serve one another. But what made the difference in the upper room and in everything that Jesus did? He did only what His Father told Him, remaining in complete dependence moment by moment.

- "Jesus knew that the Father had put all things under his power, and that he had come from God and was returning to God; so . . ."
- Jesus knew His identity in God, so . . .
- He knew where He came from and where He was going, so . . .

Because He knew His identity and His origin and His ultimate destination, He was freed from the opinions of others. He could serve and show unselfish love to His disciples even when it went against the world's norm. When we truly have a dependence on God we have a new identity, an identity not centered in what we can get for ourselves but centered in what He asks of us and in what we are in Him.

This is one of the truly freeing things about dependence. We are freed from the grip of the selfish "I did it my way" to follow the example of Jesus in "doing it His way." This and only this will allow us to be subservient, unconditionally loving, peaceful, and selfless under provocation.

After His demonstration of dependence, Jesus stated: "A new command I give you: Love one another. As I have loved you, so you must love one another" (verse 34). We cannot follow this command without the dependence He demonstrated throughout His life. Without dependence, we will be worrying about what others are thinking of us, or we'll be trying to get ahead of the other person instead of loving them. We need a new identity that comes only from dependence on Jesus and the Father.

I am going to paraphrase my name into John 13:3, 4, but I would like you to put your name in.

DuWayne knew that Jesus and the Father had entrusted to him great power through dependence on Them, and that he had been born from God's creative power and was to return to God, so he was empowered to selflessly serve and love.

Powerful? The wonderful part is that it is the truth, and He has promised it to us! We have come from Him and are to return to Him. We are entrusted with much power through dependence on Him. We are not fearful of the present or future because He has everything under control. We are not held captive by the expectations of the world and the struggle for personal significance. We are significant! Not in ourselves but through Jesus and His sacrifice and His work within us, we are significant. Because of that we can be free to do things His way, through dependence on Him.

What about you? Are you ready to step out of the boat of "safety and security"? Are you ready to receive a new identity, then step out in dependence on Him and what He has planned for your life? He is not calling us to comfort and routine. He is calling you and me to a place of vulnerability, where we are looking only to Him for our marching orders as well as the cadence of our marching.

CHAPTER 17

HOW DOES ONE LIVE
THE DEPENDENT LIFE?

In practical terms, how is the dependent life lived? I have been asked, "What do we have to *do* when we are depending on God? We can't just sit around and let everything happen, right?" First, our heart has to be right with God. This means that we are truly searching for God and His will. Knowingly holding on to a cherished sin that will separate me from God's presence and pleasure does not work. God promised in Jeremiah, "You will seek me and find me when you seek me with all your heart" (Jer. 29:13).

Searching must take place on a daily basis. Look for His will in the Scriptures. Pray constantly. Be in communion with God on a frequent basis, asking for His will in all decisions. Humbly approach God in the experiential knowledge that you are incapable of doing His will on your own—the basic distrust of yourself.

Maintain the joyful attitude He wants from us. When irritation or anxiety pops up, step back and evaluate whether you are truly being dependent in the situation. Likely the answer is "no" if you're experiencing frustration or worry. Stop, recommit, and evaluate your humility, whether you are allowing God to be Lord, whether you are submitting to God's will, and whether you are listening to God's call. Corrections and readjustments are made through prayer and asking for God's power to change the problem areas. Temptations and conflicts can be met with a grateful attitude for personal growth if we meet them in God's power and for His glory, not our own.

When we have no idea what His will is, we must be listening for His will to be revealed and remain willing to act or wait according to the direction given. God can speak through that still small voice of our conscience. But He does have different venues through which He reveals His plan. One common way He speaks is through Scripture. Many guidelines for living are laid down in His Word.

"The one who is unwilling to work shall not eat" (2 Thess. 3:10).

"Anyone who does not provide for their relatives . . . has denied the faith and is worse than an unbeliever" (1 Tim. 5:8).

"The borrower is slave to the lender" (Prov. 22:7).

Fortunately, God does not tell us one thing in His Word and another in our impressions or through godly friends. I've been told of decisions that someone believed were from God and yet things didn't work out—marriages entered into outside of God's scriptural direction, purchases made that pushed the individual into deeper debt in spite of biblical counsel against borrowing, etc. If we are truly depending on God and not pushing our agenda, we need to take into consideration all the areas in which He speaks to us.

If there are discrepancies from what we think we are hearing from others or in our conscience with what is found in the Scriptures, we must proceed very cautiously to find out why before deciding what really is God's will. God never gives direction that contradicts what is outlined in Scripture.

It is always easier to depend on God when we realize it is not possible to rely on our self. This became very evident to me when I took my family on a medical mission trip to Kabul, Afghanistan, in early 2009. Americans were targets for the Taliban and other insurgents. There was no way for me to protect my family on my own. I *had* to rely on God's protective power. I felt He had called us to go and we knew that He would work everything out, not necessarily the way we wanted, but definitely for His purposes. Thankfully, He gave us a safe trip.

Paul also found dependence easier when he couldn't rely on himself, as he writes in 2 Corinthians 12:7-10:

"God knows how naturally subject to pride I am, so to keep me humble and dependent on Him, He has allowed me to continue to have poor eyesight and other bodily weaknesses. These infirmities are like a thorn in the flesh which Satan uses to beat my spirit to the ground, yet this is what keeps me from being too independent, which I tend to be. . . . 'Your handicap will make you depend on me, and that's when you'll be the strongest'" (Clear Word).

I know I have already spoken to the men, but I must reiterate. I perceive that it is much harder for men to learn humility, their need of help, and submission than it is for women. The independent spirit in men is fostered even more by our society. The devil knows that as the head of the household, a man with a dependent spirit will change the whole family. A true life conversion for the man will influence the wife and even rebelling teenagers. Look at the percentages of church attendance in Christian churches. Women are more likely to be in church than men. Why? Men often don't feel they need God.

Men especially need more than a philosophical assent to God's sovereignty. "These people come near to me with their mouth and honor me with their lips, but their hearts are far from me" (Isa. 29:13). Where is your heart? Are you ready to experience peace from your fears or relief from your depression? How about victory in crossing your Red Sea, clearing "giants" from your land, or scaling insurmountable heights? Triumph comes when we "step out of the boat'" into dependence. Hang on for the ride as we follow Him to the Promised Land.

It was two weeks before our first Lincoln half marathon. The cool, sunny day was perfect for running, but we were nearing mile 11, the hilly section of the run, with a mild headwind. My son Brad had been struggling through much of the mileage and was drafting me (running behind so as to avoid some of the wind) going up the first two hills. My quads were screaming and I was getting winded, breathing at twice my normal running rate. I knew I'd had it.

I gasped to Brad that I was going only 12.25 miles, eliminating the last .85 miles that constituted the half-marathon mileage. He immediately surged out into the lead and called over his shoulder, "Come on, Dad, you can make it."

I was not so sure. Although we were 22 seconds ahead of the eight-minute-per-mile pace we'd set as our goal, it would hurt, and hurt bad, if we were going to finish. I asked the Lord for help and tried to pick up the pace. There were three more hills to conquer. We struggled to maintain pace, ignoring our fatigue.

Two hills down, we rounded the corner for the last quarter mile with 1:08 minutes left. I knew I wouldn't quite make the time, but still pushed as hard as I could. At 105 minutes 8 seconds, I finished the training run. I had made it through the pain and fatigue, overcoming the barriers to a successful finish! Granted, it wasn't quite the finish I wanted, but I didn't quit, even when I desperately wanted to.

In reality that is exactly how it is with our dependence on God. It isn't easy maintaining a constant humble, depending willingness. When irritations present, especially several at once, life seems insurmountable and it's tempting to quit. Jesus, though, is running just ahead and encouraging us, *"You can do this. It is possible to maintain your dependence even when you don't think you can do it. Just look at My example. Hang in there! I know it isn't quite the way you had envisioned it, but hold on to Me and finish in My strength."*

CHOICES

Even after all of the amazing victories over the Canaanites, the children of Israel still questioned God's wonderful providence. The people of Joseph approached Joshua, saying,

"'Why have you given us only one allotment and one portion for an inheritance? We are a numerous people, and the Lord has blessed us abundantly.'

"'If you are so numerous,' Joshua answered, 'and if the hill country of Ephraim is too small for you, go up into the forest and clear land for yourselves there in the land of the Perizzites and Rephaites.'

"The people of Joseph replied, 'The hill country is not enough for us, and all the Canaanites who live in the plain have chariots fitted with iron, both those in Beth Shan and in its settlements and those in the Valley of Jezreel.'

"But Joshua said to the tribes of Joseph—to Ephraim and Manasseh— 'You are numerous and very powerful. You will have not only one allotment but the forested hill country as well. Clear it, and its farthest limits will be yours; though the Canaanites have chariots fitted with iron and though they are strong, you can drive them out'" (Joshua 17:14-18).

They had seen what God would do for them, how He gave them cities they did not have to build and vineyards they did not have to plant; how He granted victory over the Canaanites without losing soldiers and sometimes with very little effort on their part. Yet they still did not depend on His providence to give them their full allotment of the land.

Caleb, on the other hand, had a fully different view of his purpose and conquest in the Promised Land. "Caleb's faith now was just what it was when his testimony had contradicted the evil report of the spies. He had believed God's promise that He would put His people in possession of Canaan, and in this he had followed the Lord fully. . . . Amid all the hardships, perils, and plagues of the desert wanderings, and during the years of warfare since entering Canaan, the Lord had preserved him; and now at upwards of fourscore his vigor was unabated. He did not ask for himself a land already conquered, but the place which above all others the spies had thought it impossible to subdue. By the help of God he would wrest his stronghold from the very giants whose power had staggered the faith of Israel. It was no desire for honor or aggrandizement that prompted Caleb's request. The brave old warrior was desirous of giving to the people an example that would honor God, and encourage the tribes fully to subdue the land which their fathers had deemed unconquerable.

"Caleb obtained the inheritance upon which his heart had been set for forty years, and, trusting in God to be with him, he 'drove thence the three sons of Anak.' Having thus secured a possession for himself and his house, his zeal did not abate; he did not settle down to enjoy his inheritance, but pushed on to further conquests for the benefit of the nation and the glory of God.

"The cowards and rebels had perished in the wilderness, but the righteous spies ate of the grapes of Eschol. To each was given according to his faith. The unbelieving had seen their fears fulfilled. Notwithstanding God's promise, they had declared that it was impossible to inherit Canaan, and they did not possess it. But those who trusted in God, looking not so much to the difficulties to be encountered as to the strength of their Almighty Helper, entered the goodly land" (*Patriarchs and Prophets*, p. 513).

At the end of the formal conquest of the Promised Land, Joshua summoned the leaders of the tribes of Israel. He reminded them of all that God had done for them since the time of Abraham right down to the conquering of the Canaanites.

"Now fear the Lord and serve him with all faithfulness. Throw away the gods your ancestors worshiped beyond the Euphrates River and in Egypt, and serve the Lord. But if serving the Lord seems undesirable to you, then choose for yourselves this day whom you will serve, whether the gods your ancestors served beyond the Euphrates, or the gods of the Amorites, in whose land you are living. But as for me and my household, we will serve the Lord" (Joshua 24:14, 15).

How about you? God has demonstrated His love for you. He has shown you that He wants to be with you continually and wants more than anything for you to be fully dependent on His ability to continue to lead you toward happiness and His Promised Land for you. Are you going to worship the gods of your ancestors—wealth, power, prestige, personal significance outside of God, independence from God? Or are you going to serve the One who has led and wants to lead you further on the path to Him? "Choose for yourselves this day whom you will serve, whether the gods your ancestors served beyond the Euphrates, or the gods of the Amorites, in whose land you are living. But as for me and my household, we will serve the Lord" (verse 15).

May your journey to dependence be met with all of the blessings that He has promised for you, both here and in the Promised Land. Ephesians 3:20 says, "Now to him who is able to do immeasurably more than all we ask or imagine, according to his power that is at work within us." Yes, immeasurably more than all we ask or imagine is what He promises. I pray that you will allow Him to see you, in ways that are immeasurably more than all we ask or imagine, through the encounters with the giants in the land, whatever they may be in your life, and that we each will meet and depend on our Savior now, and soon, face to face.

I do not write this manuscript to get you to make a mental assent that, "Yes, God wants dependence from me." Please consciously make this a daily prayer and constant striving to make the decision to remain fully dependent on Him. Eliminate the things that are keeping you from depending on Him, especially pride and selfishness. Accept His gift on the cross and follow His example of complete dependence on the Father. Through that dependence gain the peace He has promised and then live the abundant life, which is unaffected by the circumstances of the world.

Please do not let it be said about you as it was about the Israelites: "These people come near to me with their mouth and honor me with their lips, but their hearts are far from me" (Isa. 29:13). Join David in saying, "The Lord has become my fortress, and my God the rock in whom I take refuge" (Ps. 94:22).

Remember what was quoted from *Patriarchs and Prophets*: "To each was given according to his faith." If our faith is expecting the worst and not relying on God, we will see the worst happen to us (missing the peace, rest, freedom, and then the Promised Land). If we are depending on His strength fully and are acting accordingly, as Caleb and Joshua did, we will see that Promised Land and have all the benefits in the present as well.

God is gathering a people who are willing to depend on Him fully for the last days of this world's history. Remember that at Christ's first coming, only Simeon and Anna recognized Jesus in the Temple. Both recognized Him through the prompting of the Spirit. Jesus said that in the last days it will be very hard to distinguish between truth and error, "to deceive, if possible, even the elect" (Matt. 24:24). Revelation 14:12 says that the saints will have the "faith of Jesus" (KJV). These saints will be depending completely on God's Spirit for guidance, as Jesus did. They will be those "elect" who will not be deceived. They are the ones that will expectantly and triumphantly see Jesus appearing in the clouds.

JESUS' DEPENDENCE

"Very truly I tell you, the Son can do nothing by himself; he can do only what he sees his Father doing, because whatever the Father does the Son also does. For the Father loves the Son and shows him all he does" (John 5:19, 20).

"By myself I can do nothing; I judge only as I hear, and my judgment is just, for I seek not to please myself but him who sent me" (verse 30).

"For I have come down from heaven not to do my will but to do the will of him who sent me" (John 6:38).

"My teaching is not my own. It comes from the one who sent me" (John 7:16).

"When you have lifted up the Son of Man, then you will know that I am he and that I do nothing on my own but speak just what the Father has taught me. The one who sent me is with me; he has not left me alone, for I always do what pleases him" (John 8:28, 29).

"For I did not speak on my own, but the Father who sent me commanded me to say all that I have spoken. I know that his command leads to eternal life. So whatever I say is just what the Father has told me to say" (John 12:49, 50).

"The words I say to you I do not speak on my own authority. Rather, it is the Father, living in me, who is doing his work" (John 14:10).

"If you keep my commands, you will remain in my love, just as I have kept my Father's commands and remain in his love" (John 15:10).

"Christ suffered for you, leaving you an example, that you should follow in his steps. 'He committed no sin, and no deceit was found in his mouth.' When they hurled their insults at him, he did not retaliate; when he suffered, he made no threats. Instead, he entrusted himself to him who judges justly" (1 Peter 2:21-23).

DEPENDENCE

"The 'honest and good heart' of which the parable speaks, is not a heart without sin; for the gospel is to be preached to the lost. Christ said, 'I came not to call the righteous, but sinners to repentance.' Mark 2:17. He has an honest heart who yields to the conviction of the Holy Spirit. He confesses his guilt, and feels his need of the mercy and love of God. He has a sincere desire to know the truth, that he may obey it. The good heart is a believing heart, one that has faith in the word of God" (*Christ's Object Lessons*, pp. 58, 59).

"A knowledge of the truth depends not so much upon strength of intellect as upon pureness of purpose, the simplicity of an earnest, dependent faith. To those who in humility of heart seek for divine guidance, angels of God draw near. The Holy Spirit is given to open to them the rich treasures of the truth. The good-ground hearers, having heard the word, keep it. Satan with all his agencies of evil is not able to catch it away" (*ibid.*, p. 59).

"Whenever man accomplishes anything, whether in spiritual or in temporal lines, he should bear in mind that he does it through cooperation with his Maker. There is great necessity for us to realize our dependence on God. Too much confidence is placed in man, too much reliance on human inventions. There is too little confidence in the power that God stands ready to give. 'We are laborers together with God' (1 Cor. 3:9). Immeasurably inferior is the part that the human agent sustains; but if he is linked with the divinity of Christ, he can do all things through the strength that Christ imparts" (*ibid.*, p. 82).

"But many have not a living faith. This is why they do not see more of the power of God. Their weakness is the result of their unbelief. They have more faith in their own working than in the working of God for them. They take themselves into their own keeping. They plan and devise, but pray little, and have little real trust in God. They think they have faith, but it is only the impulse of the moment. Failing to realize their own need, or God's willingness to give, they do not persevere in keeping their requests before the Lord" (*ibid.*, p. 145).

"We need to have far less confidence in what man can do and far more confidence in what God can do for every believing soul. He longs to have you reach after Him by faith. He longs to have you expect great things from Him. He longs to give you understanding in temporal as well as in spiritual matters. He can sharpen the intellect. He can give tact and skill. Put your talents into the work, ask God for wisdom, and it will be given you" (*ibid.*, p. 146).

"As activity increases and men become successful in doing any work for God, there is danger of trusting to human plans and methods. There is a tendency to pray less, and to have less faith. Like the disciples, we are in danger of losing sight of our dependence on God, and seeking to make a savior of our activity. We need to look constantly to Jesus, realizing that it is His power that does the work. While we are to labor earnestly for the salvation of the lost, we must also take time for meditation, for prayer, and for the study of the word of God. Only the work accomplished with much prayer, and sanctified by the merit of Christ, will in the end prove to have been efficient for good" (*The Desire of Ages,* p. 362).

"He [Jesus] must turn aside from a life of ceaseless activity and contact with human needs, to seek retirement and unbroken communion with His Father. As one with us, a sharer in our needs and weaknesses, He was wholly dependent upon God, and in the secret place of prayer He sought divine strength, that He might go forth braced for duty and trial. . . . Through continual communion He received life from God, that He might impart life to the world. His experience is to be ours" (*ibid.,* p. 363).

"In all who are under the training of God is to be revealed a life that is not in harmony with the world, its customs, or its practices; and everyone needs to have a personal experience in obtaining a knowledge of the will of God. We must individually hear Him speaking to the heart. When every other voice is hushed, and in quietness we wait before Him, the silence of the soul makes more distinct the voice of God. He bids us, 'Be still, and know that I am God.' Ps. 46:10. Here alone can true rest be found. And this is the effectual preparation for all who labor for God. Amid the hurrying throng, and the strain of life's intense activities, the soul that is thus refreshed will be surrounded with an atmosphere of light and peace. The life will breathe out fragrance, and will reveal a divine power that will reach men's hearts" (*ibid.*).

"The providence of God had placed Jesus where He was; and He depended on His heavenly Father for the means to relieve the necessity. And when we are brought into strait places, we are to depend on God. We are to exercise wisdom and judgment in every action of life, that we may not, by reckless movements, place ourselves in trial. We are not to plunge into difficulties, neglecting the means God has provided, and misusing the faculties He has given us. Christ's workers are to obey His instructions implicitly. The work is God's, and if we would bless others His plans must be followed. Self cannot be made a center; self can receive no honor" (*ibid.,* pp. 368, 369).

"The means in our possession may not seem to be sufficient for the work; but if we will move forward in faith, believing in the all-sufficient power of God, abundant resources will open before us. If the work be of God, He Himself will provide the means for its accomplishment. He will reward honest, simple reliance upon Him. The little that is wisely and economically used in the service of the Lord of heaven will increase in the very act of imparting. In the hand of Christ the small supply of food remained undiminished until the famished multitude were satisfied. If we go to the Source of all strength, with our hands of faith outstretched to receive, we shall be sustained in our work, even under the most forbidding circumstances, and shall be enabled to give to others the bread of life" (*ibid.*, p. 371).

Hebrews 13:5, 6 provides supporting light to wealth and dependence on God: "Keep your lives free from the love of money and be content with what you have, because God has said, 'Never will I leave you, never will I forsake you.' So we say with confidence, 'The Lord is my helper; I will not be afraid. What can mere mortals do to me?'"

When taken in context, this text echoes what Christ told the rich young ruler. "Don't depend on your wealth because there is no security there. Instead, depend on Me and I will be your helper. Do not be afraid because I will be with you and will never forsake you."

"Remember how the Lord your God led you all the way in the wilderness these forty years, to humble and test you in order to know what was in your heart, whether or not you would keep his commands. He humbled you, causing you to hunger and then feeding you with manna, which neither you nor your ancestors had known, to teach you that man does not live on bread alone but on every word that comes from the mouth of the Lord. Your clothes did not wear out and your feet did not swell during these forty years. Know then in your heart that as a man disciplines his son, so the Lord your God disciplines you" (Deut. 8:2-5).

Moses appears to state that humanity also lives through dependence on God and hearing His words.

"The Lord will vindicate his people and relent concerning his servants when he sees their strength is gone and no one is left, slave or free. He will say: 'Now where are their gods, the rock they took refuge in, the gods who ate the fat of their sacrifices and drank the wine of their drink offerings? Let them rise up to help you! Let them give you shelter! See now that I myself am he! There is no god besides me. . . . Take to heart all the words I have solemnly declared to you this day, so that you may command your children to obey carefully all the words of this law. They are not just idle words for you—*they are your life*'" (Deut. 32:36-47).

What is your life? Understand that God is sovereign, that He wants to be your refuge and defender, that He wants you to listen to Him and allow Him to circumcise your heart.

"Cursed is the one who trusts in man, who draws strength from mere flesh and whose heart turns away from the Lord. That person will be like a bush in the wastelands; they will not see prosperity when it comes. They will dwell in the parched places of the desert, in a salt land where no one lives. But blessed is the one who trusts in the Lord, whose confidence is in him. They will be like a tree planted by the water that sends out its roots by the stream. It does not fear when heat comes; its leaves are always green. It has no worries in a year of drought and never fails to bear fruit" (Jer. 17:5-8).

"No one who hopes in me ever regrets it" (Isa. 49:23, Message).

"Let the one who walks in the dark, who has no light, trust in the name of the Lord and rely on their God" (Isa. 50:10).

"My salvation and my honor depend on God; he is my mighty rock, my refuge. Trust in him at all times, you people; pour out your hearts to him, for God is our refuge" (Ps. 62:7, 8).

"Though the fig tree does not bud and there are no grapes on the vines, though the olive crop fails and the fields produce no food, though there are no sheep in the pen and no cattle in the stalls, yet I will rejoice in the Lord, I will be joyful in God my Savior. The Sovereign Lord is my strength; he makes my feet like the feet of a deer, he enables me to tread on the heights" (Hab. 3:17-19).

"When calamity comes, the wicked are brought down, but even in death the righteous seek refuge in God" (Prov. 14:32). Yes, even in death (the worst thing many can think of) the righteous have a refuge.

"The Lord's unfailing love surrounds the one who trusts in him" (Ps. 32:10).

"No one who takes refuge in him will be condemned" (Ps. 34:22).

"People take refuge in the shadow of your wings" (Ps. 36:7).

"The salvation of the righteous comes from the Lord: he is their stronghold in time of trouble. The Lord helps them and delivers them; he delivers them from the wicked and saves them, because they take refuge in him" (Ps. 37:39, 40).

"Do not worry about your life, what you will eat or drink; or about your body, what you will wear. . . . Look at the birds of the air; they do not sow or reap or store away in barns, and yet your heavenly Father feeds them. Are you not much more valuable than they? . . . And why do you worry about clothes? See how the flowers of the field grow. They do not labor or spin. Yet I tell you that not even Solomon in all his splendor was dressed like one of these. If that is how God clothes the grass of the field, which is here today and tomorrow is thrown into the fire, will he not much more clothe you—you of little faith? . . . But seek first his kingdom and his righteousness, and all these things will be given to you as well" (Matt. 6:25-33).

"Growth in grace will not lead you to be proud, self-confident, and boastful, but will make you more conscious of your own nothingness, and of your entire dependence upon the Lord" (*God's Amazing Grace*, p. 296).

HUMILITY/PRIDE

"The spirit of the slothful servant we are often fain to call humility. But true humility is widely different. To be clothed with humility does not mean that we are to be dwarfs in intellect, deficient in aspiration, and cowardly in our lives, shunning burdens lest we fail to carry them successfully. Real humility fulfills God's purposes by depending upon His strength" (*Christ's Object Lessons*, p. 363).

"We need to shun everything that would encourage pride and self-sufficiency; therefore we should beware of giving or receiving flattery or praise. It is Satan's work to flatter. He deals in flattery as well as in accusing and condemnation. Thus he seeks to work the ruin of the soul. Those who give praise to men are used by Satan as his agents. Let the workers for Christ direct every word of praise away from themselves. Let self be put out of sight. Christ alone is to be exalted" (*ibid.*, p. 161).

"The Lord your God will circumcise your hearts and the hearts of your descendants, so that you may love him with all your heart and with all your soul, and live" (Deut. 30:6). Circumcision of the heart is nothing but removing our pride, selfishness, and arrogance. Only with these things circumcised from our hearts will we be able to truly love Him with all our heart and soul.

"There are six things which the Lord hates, seven which are an abomination to him: haughty eyes" (Prov. 6:16, 17, RSV).

Pride and arrogance are condemned a number of times in Proverbs:

"The fear of the Lord is hatred of evil. Pride and arrogance and the way of evil and perverted speech I hate" (Prov. 8:13, RSV).

"When pride comes, then comes disgrace: but with the humble is wisdom" (Prov. 11:2, RSV).

"Pride goes before destruction, and a haughty spirit before a fall" (Prov. 16:18, RSV).

"Whoever lives by the truth comes into the light, so that it may be seen plainly that what they have done has been done in the sight of God" (John 3:21). In other words, when we live by the truth (that we can do everything through Him but nothing without Him), our lives make it plain that our successes come through Him and not through ourselves.

GOD'S SOVEREIGNTY AND MY NEED OF IT

"In the future, when your son asks you, 'What is the meaning of the stipulations, decrees, and laws the Lord our God has commanded you?' tell him: 'We were slaves of Pharaoh in Egypt, but the Lord brought us out of Egypt with a mighty hand. Before our eyes the Lord sent signs and wonders—great and terrible—on Egypt and Pharaoh and his whole household. But he brought us out from there to bring us in and give us the land he promised on oath to our ancestors. The Lord commanded us to obey all these decrees and to fear the Lord our God, so that we might always prosper and be kept alive, as is the case today. And if we are careful to obey all this law before the Lord our God, as he has commanded us, that will be our righteousness'" (Deut. 6:20-25). This is a text that could be used to support pharisaical lawkeeping if one did not understand it from a dependence point of view.

"To the Lord your God belong the heavens, even the highest heavens, the earth and everything in it. Yet the Lord set his affection on your ancestors and loved them, and he chose you, their descendants, above all the nations—as it is today. Circumcise your hearts, therefore, and do not be stiff-necked any longer. For the Lord your God is God of gods and Lord of lords, the great God, mighty and awesome, who shows no partiality and accepts no bribes. He defends the cause of the fatherless and the widow, and loves the foreigner residing among you, giving them food and clothing. And you are to love those who are foreigners, for you yourselves were foreigners in Egypt. Fear the Lord your God and serve him. Hold fast to him and take your oaths in his name. He is the one you praise; he is your God, who performed for you those great and awesome wonders you saw with your own eyes" (Deut. 10:14-21).

"They will have no fear of bad news; their hearts are steadfast, trusting in the Lord. Their hearts are secure, they will have no fear; in the end they will look in triumph on their foes" (Ps. 112:7, 8).

"For the eyes of the Lord range throughout the earth to strengthen those whose hearts are fully committed to him" (2 Chron. 16:9).

"'Not by might nor by power, but by my Spirit,' says the Lord Almighty" (Zech. 4:6).

LOOKING FOR AND SUBMITTING TO GOD'S WILL

"These are rebellious people, deceitful children, children unwilling to listen to the Lord's instruction" (Isa. 30:9).

"Do not be stiff-necked, as your ancestors were; submit to the Lord" (2 Chron. 30:8).

"But my people would not listen to me; Israel would not submit to me. So I gave them over to their stubborn hearts to follow their own devices" (Ps. 81:11, 12).

"Do whatever he tells you" (John 2:5). This statement by Mary to the servants at the wedding in Cana represents what we need to do all the time. Sometimes what He tells us to do is found in Scripture. Sometimes it is through the Holy Spirit that He reveals His wishes. Whatever methods He uses to reveal His will, just do it. When we obey through His strength, miracles happen, as at the wedding. The servants did exactly what He told them, and the miracle followed. Direct obedience leads to miracles.

"The mind governed by the flesh is death, but the mind governed by the Spirit is life and peace. The mind governed by the flesh is hostile to God; it does not submit to God's law, nor can it do so. Those who are in the realm of the flesh cannot please God. You, however, are not in the realm of the flesh but are in the realm of the Spirit, if indeed the Spirit of God lives in you" (Rom. 8:6-9).

LISTENING TO GOD'S VOICE

"Now choose life, so that you and your children may live and that you may love the Lord your God, listen to his voice, and hold fast to him. For *the Lord is your life*" (Deut. 30:19, 20).

"Go near to listen rather than to offer the sacrifice of fools" (Eccl. 5:1). Don't go near to God to give Him something. Go near to hear Him.

"Listen! I am going to bring on this city and all the villages around it every disaster I pronounced against them, because they were stiff-necked and would not listen to my words" (Jer. 19:15).

"His sheep follow him because they know his voice. . . . They do not recognize a stranger's voice" (John 10:4, 5).

"I am the good shepherd; I know my sheep and my sheep know me" (verse 14).

'My sheep listen to my voice; I know them, and they follow me" (verse 27).

WAITING ON THE LORD

"He who believes will not be in haste" (Isa. 28:16, RSV).

"Those who wait for me shall not be put to shame" (Isa. 49:23, RSV).

"Wait for the Lord; be strong and take heart and wait for the Lord" (Ps. 27:14). Waiting on the Lord is not for the faint of heart, but David encourages us to "be strong and take heart," because things will always work out for our best if we do wait for the Lord!

"Those who hope in the Lord will renew their strength. They will soar on wings like eagles; they will run and not grow weary, they will walk and not be faint" (Isa. 40:31).

PEACE AND REST

"The Lord your God is with you, the Mighty Warrior who saves. He will take great delight in you; in his love he will no longer rebuke you, but will rejoice over you with singing" (Zeph. 3:17).

"You shall not seek their peace or their prosperity all your days for ever" (Deut. 23:6, RSV).

"The Lord gives strength to his people; the Lord blesses his people with peace" (Ps. 29:11).

"The meek will inherit the land and enjoy peace and prosperity" (Ps. 37:11).

"A heart at peace gives life to the body" (Prov. 14:30).

"I have told you these things, so that in me you may have peace. In this world you will have trouble. But take heart! I have overcome the world" (John 16:33).

RESULTS OF OUR DEPENDENCE

"Now when all the Amorite kings west of the Jordan and all the Canaanite kings along the coast heard how the Lord had dried up the Jordan before the Israelites until they had crossed over, their hearts melted in fear and they no longer had the courage to face the Israelites" (Joshua 5:1).

"The fear of God came on all the surrounding kingdoms when they heard how the Lord had fought against the enemies of Israel. And the kingdom of Jehoshaphat was at peace, for his God had given him rest on every side" (2 Chron. 20:29, 30). When God is able to work through us because we are depending on Him, others notice and realize that He is God.

What Good Leaders Know

Ted N. C. Wilson
Charles Bradford
Cindy Tutsch
Dan Jackson
Lowell Cooper
Delbert Baker
Prudence LaBeach Pollard
Gordon Bietz
Jim Gilley
Leslie Pollard
Gerry Karst
Derek Morris
Willie and Elaine Oliver
David Smith
Sung Kwon
Ivan Leigh Warden
Ella Simmons
Pardon Mwansa
David S. Penner
Lilya Wagner,
with Halvard Thomsen

As I Follow Christ

Whether you're leading in a ministry, an organization, or a family, God has given you a special mission. *As I Follow Christ* helps you fulfill that mission with excellence. In this book some of the most notable leaders in the Seventh-day Adventist Church share what they've learned about effective leadership from their own experience, the Bible, and the Spirit of Prophecy. They describe:

- What kind of person God calls to lead
- What leaders can learn from failure
- The key elements of a leader's spiritual life
- How to set priorities and family time
- The role of accountability and discipline in the life of a leader

If you want to influence people and inspire positive change, open these pages and discover the principles that are practiced by our most outstanding leaders. Hardcover. 978-0-8280-2724-3

dventistBookCenter.com | 800.765.6955

R **Review&Herald**®
Spread the Word

This Could Change Everything

Find transforming power for your life

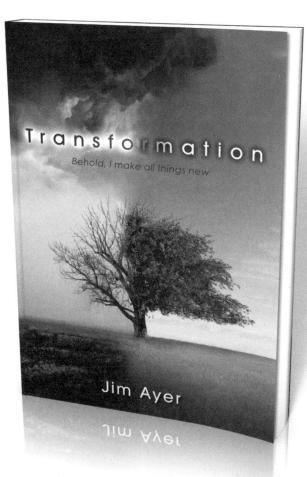

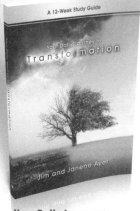

Your Daily Journey to Transformation
A 12-week Study Guide
Paperback
978-0-8280-2702-1

Remodeling Your Life DVD
God's Transforming Power
Jim Ayer's TV series on DVD.
Twelve 30-minute episodes.
3-DVD set.
978-0-8280-2746-5

Do you feel like temptations always beat you into submission? You can't seem to win a victory and wonder if you're not trying hard enough, or if God isn't holding up His end of the bargain.

In the book, *Transformation*, Jim Ayer opens up about his own experience as a serial sinner and tells how he connected with the power that God has provided to change us from the inside out.

A companion study guide, *Your Daily Journey to Transformation*, Jim and Janene Ayer take individuals or small groups on a 12-week journey toward a transformed life—a life shaped and energized by the Holy Spirit.

"Behold, I make all things new," says Jesus. See that promise fulfilled in your life today.
Paperback, 978-0-8280-2711-3

Availability subject to change.

Review&Herald
Spread the Word